D1713928

Sporting
Lives

SPORTS AND AMERICAN CULTURE SERIES
Bruce Clayton, Editor

Sporting *Lives*

• • • •

METAPHOR AND MYTH

IN AMERICAN SPORTS

AUTOBIOGRAPHIES

JAMES W. PIPKIN

UNIVERSITY OF MISSOURI PRESS
COLUMBIA AND LONDON

University of Missouri Press, Columbia, Missouri 65201
Printed and bound in the United States of America

Library of Congress Cataloging-in-Publication Data

Pipkin, James W., 1944–
    Sporting lives : metaphor and myth in American sports autobiographies / James W. Pipkin.
        p.   cm. — (Sports and American culture series)
    Summary: "Examines autobiographies by athletes such as Wilt Chamberlain, Babe Ruth, Martina Navratilova, and Dennis Rodman, and analyzes common themes and recurring patterns in the accounts of their lives and sporting experiences"—Provided by publisher.
        Includes bibliographical references and index.
        ISBN 978-0-8262-1779-0 (alk. paper)
    1. Athletes—United States—Biography.   2. Autobiographies—United States.
3. Sports—United States—Biography.   I. Title.
    GV697.A1P475 2008
    796.092'273—dc22
    [B]

                                                                    2007042564

Jacket Designer: Aaron Lueders
Page Designer: Stephanie Foley
Typesetter: BookComp, Inc.
Printer and binder: The Maple-Vail Book Manufacturing Group
Typefaces: Optima and Palatino

The University of Missouri Press acknowledges the generous contributions provided by the Martha Gano Houstoun Endowment through the Department of English at the University of Houston, and by Dean John Antel of the College of Liberal Arts and Social Sciences, University of Houston, toward the publication of this book.

For Roberta

AND

In memory of my mother,
Kate Jackson Pipkin

Contents

• • • • • • • • • • • • *Acknowledgments*

I want to thank Wyman Herendeen, the chairman of the Department of English at the University of Houston, for the administrative support he provided for me when I was researching and writing this book. He and his predecessors as chair, John McNamara and Terrell Dixon, have worked hard to foster faculty scholarship and still emphasize the importance of commitment to teaching.

I also want to acknowledge grant support from the department's Martha Gano Houstoun Endowment and from Dean John Antel of the College of Liberal Arts and Social Sciences.

I am particularly grateful to my colleagues William Monroe, Robert Phillips, and James Pickering, who read my manuscript and offered thoughtful comments and suggestions, along with support and encouragement.

My colleagues and friends, Lawrence Curry, Jr., and John Lienhard, and my former student and assistant editor for a university press, Thomas Fenske, provided advice and encouragement at important stages in the writing of the book.

I hope that other writers who submit their manuscripts to a press receive the kind of support and generosity that Beverly Jarrett, the director and editor-in-chief of the University of Missouri Press, and Bruce Clayton, the editor of the Press's Sports and American Culture Series, have given to me. I also thank John Brenner for his close and thoughtful copyediting of the manuscript.

I feel a much deeper gratitude to my wife and colleague, Roberta Weldon, and my children, Emily and Michael. Roberta always found that perfect balance of critical intelligence and supportive love that I needed, even while writing her own book and being a wonderful mother to our children.

Sporting
Lives

• • • • • • • •   Inside the Lines

IN THE OPENING OF HIS AUTOBIOGRAPHY *A FALSE SPRING*, Pat Jordan sits at a desk in his home in Connecticut looking at a picture of himself and Hall of Fame pitcher Warren Spahn at County Stadium in Milwaukee, Wisconsin. The photograph was taken in 1959 and the then-eighteen-year-old Jordan had just signed a professional baseball contract with the Milwaukee Braves. As he writes, it is thirteen years since that photograph was taken, and ten years since Jordan ended his baseball career without ever reaching the major leagues. He thinks of his older brother George, who played an important role in helping him as a young pitcher and who still keeps a copy of the photograph hanging on the wall of his law office. Jordan realizes that time has not altered George's pride in him or his image of the young athlete he once was. For George, it is a picture "whose lines have . . . become etched in his memory." What George cannot see lies *inside* the lines. He never saw Pat pitch in the minors, never saw the failures that made all his promise a "false spring." George "never saw those lines erased during [Pat's] years in the minor leagues and then somehow redrawn." For Jordan, writing the autobiography required "sorting and resorting those bits and pieces" of his sports career so that he could "flesh out that design" of who he is.[1]

Since Jordan never made it to the majors or became the subject of a biography, we have only his subjective view of who he is. On the other hand, our view of successful and famous athletes is somewhat like that of Pat Jordan's brother George. We have an indelible image drawn from our perspective in the stands, watching television, or reading the newspaper, but we do not know what lies beneath the

1. Pat Jordan, *A False Spring*, 8, 11.

1

surface of the public image, the sense of self as the athlete himself or herself experiences it. What Jordan's autobiography offers is not objective truth but the testimony of a participant, an interpretation of sports from the inside out.

At roughly the same time but on the other side of the continent in California, Lynda Huey was rereading her old diary as part of her preparation for writing a book about the famous male athletes she had known over the years. Huey had been a nationally competitive sprinter at San Jose State in the 1960s, and reviewing her diary made her realize that she had been a part of a dynamic era in the history of sports and had insights of her own to offer. She was also struck by several key disparities the diary revealed. In particular, she discovered hundreds of pictures of herself in her high school cheerleader's uniform but not a single photograph of her as a high school athlete. She was also surprised to find that she had chosen to remember only the fun she had in school, not the moments of doubt and alienation recorded in her diary. This moment of realization transformed her whole plan for writing a book about sports. She decided to write about *her* experience of sports, her life as an athlete and a woman, not the lives of male track stars and professional football players she had known.

As the beginning of Pat Jordan's *A False Spring* and Lynda Huey's account of the origins of her book reveal, writing a sports autobiography is about representing the self, confessing the self, and perhaps even discovering the self. In more recent books, the purpose sometimes becomes exposing the self, sensationalizing the self, and certainly in our celebrity culture marketing the self—all recurring motifs in the chorus of books that chronicle America's history as various versions of "Song of Myself." Some sports autobiographies are, in the parlance of the trade, "written with a roller"—a mechanical account of public events and on-the-field accomplishments, with the "as told to" professional writer using seemingly few personal contributions from the athlete. But many of them are much more than a paste-and-cut assemblage of great moments that culminate in "that championship season." In the best sports autobiographies, there is a clear selection process that tells a fuller and richer story offering not just facts and statistics but an interpretation. As Jordan puts it, he studied the various "bits and pieces" of his experiences until he saw a "design," a pattern. Whether the pattern is the Horatio Alger rags-to-riches story or a trajectory of rise, fall, and recovery punctuated by a trauma that provides the occasion for the triumph of the human will or spirit, the shaping energy is what Roy Pascal in his classic study of autobiography calls "a certain power of the personality over circumstance."[2]

The "power of the personality" is inseparable from the subjectivity of the autobiography, but books about sports have usually ignored this dimension of the subject, particularly the athletes' own autobiographical accounts. The typical lens for studying sports is almost always positioned *outside* the lines. Journalists have either reported the "news" in some fashion or written essays that interpreted sports from their point of view. Some of the best academic studies of sports have been written by historians and sociologists, but they tend to distrust the subjective and rely more upon the objective and empirical. The inner experience might seem to be the proper province of psychology, but contemporary scholars of psychology are even more likely than historians and sociologists to be empirical in their approach. The nature of their discipline means that social scientists do not pay much attention to the rhetorical strategies and the figurative language of metaphors and other images in sports autobiographies that capture in a very concrete way the athlete's construction of identity and the larger implications of his or her subjective experience of sports. And it is the focus on this kind of language and on key rhetorical strategies that is central to the contributions of this book.

In *Sporting Lives* I use sports autobiographies as my primary resources and the athletes' own views of their experiences as the subject of my analysis because my overriding concern is not historical accuracy or the objective reliability of the athletes' testimony but the way their subjective expressions of their experiences reflect a view of sports, one different in key respects from those written by journalists, historians, sociologists, and others who do not sit inside the lines. In addition to their lack of objectivity, another reason for the neglect of autobiographies in books about sports is the view that most athletes are not introspective and, as a result, their accounts of their lives would have very limited value. But what drives the good sports autobiographies are the stories the athletes tell, the particular episodes they select from the storehouse of their memories. Although we call

2. Roy Pascal, *Design and Truth in Autobiography*, 10.

autobiographies "life histories" and "life stories" as if those terms were exact synonyms, the best autobiographies have the qualities of a story. They emphasize not facts, but personal experiences. The factual accuracy—the historical truth—of an autobiography is important, but it is less interesting and usually less significant than the different—and deeper—kind of truth athletes reveal in telling about their experiences.

• Personal Lives as Cultural Constructions

People who decide to write their life story usually assume that they are special or unique in some way. When Lynda Huey says her review of her old diaries led her to realize, "I was being driven to *prove* I was special," she testifies to the view that all of the athletes I studied shared. Jerry Kramer, a lineman for the great Green Bay Packer football teams of the 1960s, prefaces his diary *Instant Replay* by insisting, "I'm simply not a one-dimensional figure," and then catalogues his abilities as a businessman, host of a syndicated television show, partner in a number of advertising ventures, and stock market investor. Tennis champion Alice Marble markets her life story with the blurb, "her private life was even more remarkable." Marathon swimmer Diana Nyad begins *Other Shores* with an "Author's Note" that establishes her sense of individuality: "I don't expect the reader to identify with my extremity; I only ask him to accept it." And in his autobiography *Nothing But Net*, former UCLA Bruin and Portland Trail Blazers basketball star Bill Walton quotes the Bob Dylan lyric from "Maggie's Farm," "Well I try my best to be just like I am, but everybody wants you to be just like them." Alfred Kazin has written, "The deepest side of being an American is the sense of being like nothing before us in history."[3] In the modern mass culture society in

---

3. Lynda Huey, *A Running Start: An Athlete, A Woman*, x. Jerry Kramer and Dick Schaap, *Instant Replay: The Green Bay Diary of Jerry Kramer*, xii. Alice Marble and Dale Leatherman, *Courting Danger: My Adventures in World-Class Tennis, Golden-Age Hollywood, and High-Stakes Spying*. The quotation from *Courting Danger* appears on the inside jacket cover. Marble's autobiography includes an account of her adventures as a spy for U.S. Army Intelligence during World War II when she worked undercover in Switzerland in the palatial home of a lover. Her mission was to find the names of prominent Nazis hidden in his private vault. This

which that sense of uniqueness and specialness often seems threatened, who better privileged than the lionized celebrity athlete to embody that defining cultural trait?

But there is an important paradox: despite the autobiographer's assertion of his uniqueness, his life story is representative and reverberates with broader social significance. Herbert Leibowitz, a leading scholar of American autobiography, explains this seeming contradiction by pointing to the "idealistic democratic creed" celebrated by writers like Whitman that underlies the culture's belief that in America "distinction [is] possible for anybody." Roy Pascal also agrees, arguing that "the more marked the personality, the more he seems to sum up a whole social trend, a generation, perhaps a class." The current view of history has expanded the scope of the field to include the private sphere, gender roles, and emotional life, and we are aware that cultural pressures shape our representation of personal and private life. Assumptions, for example, about the body, childhood, and play—key subjects in sports autobiographies—are cultural constructions. Writing an autobiography is in several respects a "production" of the self, and even the structures for "producing" the self are derived from cultural assumptions.[4]

Many books argue that sports are a mirror of American values while other books emphasize that sports are a world apart, but my approach in this book—interpreting sports as athletes describe their experiences from inside the lines—makes that a false distinction because the construction of the self obviously cannot escape the imprint of the culture in which the athlete lives. In his autobiography *Giant Steps*, for example, Kareem Abdul-Jabbar articulates his understanding of

---

episode culminates in her thrilling escape down a winding mountain road. While fleeing, she was shot in the back by her army contact, who, it turned out, was a double agent for the Russians. She was rescued by the colonel who headed the intelligence unit, and she recovered from her wound and returned to her tennis career after the war. Diana Nyad, *Other Shores*. Bill Walton and Gene Wojciechowski, *Nothing But Net: Just Give Me the Ball and Get Out of the Way*, 50. Alfred Kazin, "The Self in History: Reflections on Autobiography," 32.

4. Herbert Leibowitz, *Fabricating Lives: Explorations in American Autobiography*, xx. In *The Limits of Autobiography: Trauma and Testimony*, Leigh Gilmore discusses the "autobiographical paradox of the unusual or unrepresentative life becoming representative," 19. Pascal, *Design and Truth in Autobiography*, 57. For an example of literary scholarship that takes this kind of approach, see Joel Pfister, *The Production of Personal Life: Class, Gender, and the Psychological in Hawthorne's Fiction*.

the interplay between his experience of sports and his view of society in his comments about the meaning of basketball style as a style of life: "Just as white college basketball was patterned and regimented like the lives awaiting its players, the black schoolyard game demanded all the flash, guile, and individual reckless brilliance each man would need in the world facing him."[5]

The overarching structures and traditional patterns sports autobiographies use are familiar to anyone who has studied literature. It is to be expected that fiery individualists like Hall of Fame baseball players Ty Cobb and Ted Williams would cast their life stories as apologias, unrepentant and defiant testimonies to the rightness of their views of themselves, their careers, and the world. Williams announces his point of view in the title of his autobiography, *My Turn at Bat,* and Cobb's subtitle is even blunter: *The True Record.* Other autobiographies take the form of confessions: *The Dave Kopay Story: An Extraordinary Self-Revelation,* the former pro football player's account of his gradual recognition and public admission of his homosexuality; basketball player Charles Barkley's *Outrageous!* whose first chapter, "I Don't Mind Being a Jerk," sets the stage for pronouncements that range from his feelings about being marketed in college as "Boy Gorge" and "The Prince of Pizza" because of his weight to his insistence that he is no role model for the youth of America; and boxer Jake La Motta's revelations in *Raging Bull* about his violent crimes outside the ring as well as his brutal style inside it.

In other autobiographies the cultural machinery at work is found in the literary tropes and themes that provide the blueprint for the life. The bildungsroman, the novel of initiation into society, is the model for professional basketball player Chet Walker's *Long Time Coming,* which he subtitles, *A Black Man's Coming-of-Age in America,* and for NBA star Kareem Abdul-Jabbar, whose *Giant Steps* traces his development as a microcosm of the larger black consciousness movement of the 1960s and 1970s. In addition to the many conventional rags-to-riches stories, there is a subclass that adds to the pattern the cautionary tale of a "fall" and recovery. Pro basketball star Spencer Haywood's *Spencer Haywood: The Rise, the Fall, the Recovery* is typical of the genre that centers on the athlete's confessions about drug ad-

5. Kareem Abdul-Jabbar and Peter Knobler, *Giant Steps: The Autobiography of Kareem Abdul-Jabbar,* 76.

diction. In other autobiographies the crisis is some form of mental illness. Former Boston Red Sox outfielder Jim Piersall's *Fear Strikes Out*, which was made into a Hollywood movie with Anthony Perkins as Piersall and Karl Malden as his oppressive father, is perhaps the best-known example, and it also holds the distinction of being the only sports autobiography whose call number places it in the psychology section of the library.

But these conventions and patterns don't get at what is unique about the athletes' experience of sports. Some of the most striking parallels in sports autobiographies are of a very different thematic nature than the traditional literary tropes found in other autobiographies, and they are less obvious because they are usually not the overt organizing principles of the autobiographies. Instead, certain recurring motifs, sometimes fully voiced and developed but often only quietly sounded, emerged as more distinctive and illuminating constructions of the athletes' subjective experiences. The athletes' subjective experience of sports revealed the importance of childhood, the body as a site of identity, the magic of remarkable moments denied to most average people, and an unusual twist on the common fear of mortality.

- **"My Story"**

My reading of the sports autobiographies convinced me that they contained powerful cultural narratives that held broad appeal for the general reader as well as the scholar, but I realized there was a unique aspect of this particular subgenre that I needed to address. One of the most common subtitles for sports autobiographies is "My Story," but when I spoke to friends and colleagues about these autobiographies or made more formal public presentations about my research for the book, occasionally someone asked a question about authorship, about who "really" wrote these books. While it is true that some of the best sports autobiographies were written solely by the athletes themselves, most sports autobiographies are cowritten. A common suspicion, if not the assumption, is that they are all ghostwritten, that the athlete merely added a kind of autograph to the title page but contributed little else. This is clearly a legitimate issue, and it needed to be considered if I wanted to study ideas about self-image and the construction of identity, which are central subjects in the analysis of autobiographies.

A number of athletes have written their own autobiographies. It is not surprising that Bill Bradley—graduate of Princeton, Rhodes Scholar, U.S. Senator, presidential candidate—was able to draft his autobiographical *Life on the Run,* based on a diary he kept during his playing days with the New York Knicks, without the assistance of a professional writer. Marathon swimmer Diana Nyad was a Phi Beta Kappa graduate of Lake Forest College and a former doctoral student in the comparative literature program at New York University, so when she sat down in the New York Public Library to write *Other Shores* she had an unusually strong background in writing and critical thinking. The great tennis star of the 1920s, Bill Tilden, came from the "Mainline" society in Philadelphia and had already published a novel, two collections of stories, and six plays when he wrote his memoirs. Michael Oriard had left professional football and earned his Ph.D. in English at Stanford when he decided to write *The End of Autumn.* While some commentators think that he may have had an unacknowledged editor, Jack Johnson, the first black heavyweight boxing champion, writes *Jack Johnson—in the Ring—and Out* using the purple prose of a dandy that seems fitting for this Renaissance man who was a world traveler, a music hall performer, a matador in Spain, and a self-described connoisseur of the arts and women. Even though Pat Jordan says that he will always think of himself as a pitcher who happens to write rather than a writer who once happened to pitch, he had already established his career as a freelance author before his autobiography *A False Spring* appeared. And former pro football player Dave Meggysey and runner Lynda Huey had become political activists and were in residence at the Institute for the Study of Sport and Society when they wrote, respectively, *Out of Their League* and *A Running Start.*

What is also obvious about these examples is that the casual sports fan is probably familiar only with the names of Bradley and Tilden. As sole authors of their life stories, the first group of athletes I have cited are clearly the exception rather than the rule. They are also people who had meaningful careers outside of sports, and their autobiographies do not dispel the view that most sports stars—the Ty Cobbs, the Wilt Chamberlains, and the Joe Namaths—did not really write their own books. The question remains whether the more typical sports autobiography is really a kind of authorized biography rather than a true autobiography.

The most common phrases used on the title pages to describe the relationship between the athlete and the professional writer—"as told to," "with," and "and"—are not definitive, and the same phrase may not even mean the same thing to the different athletes and collaborators who use it. If we rely on the information that is sometimes provided in the preface or the foreword to the books, what seems most clear is that the professional writer is not usually a "ghost writer" who uses newspaper stories and magazine articles to create the story with little or no assistance from the athlete. The most common practice is for the professional writer to tape a series of interviews with the athlete, to write the chapters based upon the tapes, and then to submit the manuscript to the athlete for his or her input. This general process leaves a great deal of flexibility for what actually happens in a particular case.

Tennis player Pam Shriver discloses in her autobiography *Passing Shots* that her coauthor Frank Deford established a few themes and concentrated on a few main "characters" as he reviewed the diary entries she recorded. On the other hand, David Shaw insists in the "Preface" to basketball player Wilt Chamberlain's autobiography that he was really only an editor: "The words are Wilt's words. The thoughts are Wilt's thoughts. And the book is Wilt's book."[6] Chip Oliver, a former football player for the Oakland Raiders who was radicalized by the counterculture movement of the 1960s, relates that he listened to the tapes and wrote the first draft of the manuscript himself and that the main task of his coauthor, Ron Rapoport, was to edit the manuscript, primarily by deleting the highly philosophical and abstract ideas that the politically conscious Oliver imposed on his life story.

Other athletes are less specific about the exact process but nevertheless make it clear that they have an important ownership in their autobiographies. The "Acknowledgments" in *Outrageous!* describe the role of Roy S. Johnson as playing "second fiddle" to basketball star Charles Barkley in writing the autobiography, and former Los Angeles Laker Magic Johnson's "Acknowledgments" in *My Life* characterize his collaborator, William Novak, as a "point guard . . . feed-

6. Wilt Chamberlain and David Shaw, *Wilt: Just Like Any Other 7-Foot Black Millionaire Who Lives Next Door*, vi.

ing" a center.[7] These practices seem the most typical, but there is also another distinctive kind of autobiography represented by such books as Jake La Motta's *Raging Bull*, Rocky Graziano's *Somebody Up There Likes Me*, and Muhammad Ali's *The Greatest: My Own Life*, all of which are written with a novelistic technique which clearly entails more than mere editing of taped interviews.

In search of information that went beyond what could be found in the prefaces and acknowledgments of the autobiographies, I interviewed three prominent collaborators: George Vecsey, Peter Knobler, and Roy S. Johnson.

Vecsey is a longtime and distinguished columnist for the *New York Times* who has cowritten autobiographies with public figures in a variety of fields. He first worked with Loretta Lynn in the writing of *Coal Miner's Daughter,* and later collaborated with two other country singers, Barbara Mandrell and Lorrie Morgan, on their autobiographies. Most recently, he collaborated with Henry Woo, the Chinese dissident intellectual. In sports, he worked with tennis great Martina Navratilova and former Dodgers and Athletics pitcher Bob Welch on their autobiographies. Peter Knobler is a freelance writer based in New York City who has also cowritten books with people from the worlds of politics, law, sports, and other professions. He worked with Daniel Petrocelli, who represented the family of Nicole Brown Simpson in their civil lawsuit against O. J. Simpson, on *Triumph of Justice;* with political consultants James Carville and Mary Matalin on *All's Fair: Love, War, and Running for President;* with Peggy Say on *Forgotten,* an account of her struggle to free her brother Terry Anderson from an Iranian prison; and with former Texas governor Ann Richards on her autobiography, *Straight from the Heart.* He is also the coauthor of the sports autobiographies of Houston Rocket Hakeem Olajuwon (*Living the Dream*), Thomas "Hollywood" Henderson of the Dallas Cowboys (*Out of Control*), and Hall of Fame basketball player Kareem Abdul-Jabbar (*Giant Steps*). The third writer I interviewed is Roy S. Johnson, an editor at large for *Fortune,* who earlier in his career collaborated with Magic Johnson and Charles Barkley on their autobiographies. Even this brief recitation of the titles and subjects of some of their books suggests that they are not hack writ-

7. Charles Barkley and Roy S. Johnson, *Outrageous!: The Fine Life and Flagrant Good Times of Basketball's Irresistible Force.* Earvin "Magic" Johnson and William Novak, *My Life,* vii.

ers who mechanically churn out vanity pieces for celebrity clients but people with broad intellectual interests.

When I asked George Vecsey to respond to the view that athletes do not write their autobiographies, he began with the caveat that it is not in the nature of athletes to be analytical or to remember details or to put their lives into context and perspective. He quickly added that this does not mean that they are not intelligent, but rather that their training is all about performance. What his comments brought to mind was the difference between memory and what kinesiologists call "muscle memory." On the other hand, Vecsey emphasized that the professional writer's collaboration is successful only if the athlete sees the autobiography as *his* or *her* book and feels the pride of authorship. He explained that the writer brings his skills to the process, but "people have their own stories." His task is to use his abilities as an interviewer and a listener to get the athlete to open up and reveal his or her value system. His role, he continued, is "to lead, to guide." He also uses his craft to add the novelistic details that flesh out incidents in the story. In the case of Martina Navratilova's autobiography, Vecsey actually visited Prague to get a sense of the city and its sights and atmosphere and to visit Navratilova's family.

What I began to understand is that, while the athletes may not write their books in the sense that they often lack the skills to craft them, their autobiographies are authentic because they are *their stories*. For example, I asked Vecsey about the origin of some of the parts of Martina Navratilova's autobiography that I had found to be particularly interesting. In every instance I was told that the idea had originated with Navratilova. It was she who contributed the theme that she was a misfit who had finally found her home in America. It was she who introduced the subject of how she felt about her body and recounted childhood episodes in which she was mistaken for a boy. Vecsey added that he did not think she was always aware of some of the psychological implications of some of these subjects. The autobiography's concluding chapter centers on Navratilova's decision to go skiing, a sport she had loved in childhood but had given up because of the risk of an injury which might harm her tennis career. In *Martina* the event is conceptualized as a symbol of personal freedom, as a final assertion of the identity she has found as a person, a woman, and a sexual being. Interestingly, Vecsey revealed that she had not only conceived and written this chapter but had substituted it for a chapter he had written and believed to be a better conclusion for the book. These examples convinced me that Navratilova was not a passive object for the book and that it was very much her story, drawing upon her memories and her image of herself and her understanding of the meaning of her life.

Peter Knobler and I discussed Kareem Abdul-Jabbar's autobiography, *Giant Steps*, which was his first attempt at cowriting a book. Like Vecsey, he began with the observation that writing a book is a craft and there is no reason to expect an athlete or businessman or politician to possess that skill. He pointed out that no one would ask Laurence Olivier when he was going to *write* a play. "The athlete's role in the collaborative process," he said, "is the verbal equivalent of what an actor does—performance." On the other hand, he believes that the essence of autobiography is character, not issues. Autobiographies, Knobler believes, are revelations of character—what was important to the subject and how he feels about it now. "A good autobiography," he explained, "is not about policy—how to make New York safe, for example—but a story of one of twelve kids in a Boston tenement who rises to success." The job of the writer is "to get out of the way, to have the athlete tell his story to your good ear. Everything that gets in the book is clearly from them." Abdul-Jabbar made it clear to Knobler that he was more interested in religion and blackness than in basketball. These were the sources of the stories that Abdul-Jabbar felt presented his character.

Like Vecsey, Knobler conceives of himself as a listener or reader. The athletes "talk it, they tell it, they read it to make sure it's right." The writer's craft lies, first of all, in the ability to make the autobiography sound as if the athlete is speaking. If he does coin a metaphor, Knobler thinks, he has to make sure that it is within the range of the athlete. But he pointed out that many athletes are good talkers. Jabbar was very forthcoming in their collaboration on *Giant Steps*, and Knobler mentioned that "Hollywood" Henderson was such a great talker that he actually called in his story collect from prison where he was serving time for drug abuse.

The writer, Knobler continued, also has to make the tapes come alive by moving the story on like a novel. He compared his role when working with athletes who are less active talkers than Abdul-Jabbar or Henderson to that of a psychiatrist. "Some have a worldview," he explained, "but can't get it out." In those cases, he focuses on identifying patterns he hears and bringing them to the attention of the athlete.

He may ask the athlete if he wants to say what he has just said, if he is aware of the implications of what he is saying. Knobler concluded, "If I've done my job, nobody knows I'm there. I'm invisible and I've presented someone at his articulate best so that the reader thinks he's in touch with the athlete." That, he claims, is the essence of collaboration.

In my interview with Roy Johnson he touched upon the same basic issues as Vecsey and Knobler. He pointed out that we do not want to read a book by a nonwriter. Nevertheless, he said, sports autobiographies are still the athletes' books. He explained by domesticating the metaphor of the great American dream: "If I am in the market to build my dream house and can see all of its specifics, then I go to an architect and he builds it. But does that make it any less my dream house?" Unlike Vecsey and Knobler, however, Johnson conceived of his role as that of an organizer rather than a listener. He explained that in part this was because he was usually catching up with an athlete who was on the road, and he had to conduct interviews in restaurants, hotels, and locker rooms. Organization was crucial in the case of Charles Barkley because in their interviews Barkley spoke in a stream-of-consciousness style. Johnson also added that capturing the athlete's voice was an essential aspect of capturing his personality. And he mentioned, as did Vecsey and Knobler, that collaboration is a kind of match and a good match is necessary if the writer is to be able to draw the athlete out. It is the athlete's story, however. After the preliminary research, the next step in the process is sitting down with the athlete to outline the book, and for Johnson the outline is "what the athlete wants to tell."

My interviews with Vecsey, Knobler, and Johnson were not scientific research, but they reinforced the validity of the assumptions underlying my approach to the subject of sports autobiographies and what they could tell us about athletes and about American culture. I came away from the interviews with a clear sense that the book I wanted to write would be a book about stories, stories told, if not always written, by athletes whose lives reveal that we define ourselves more in the world of play than we do in the world of work.[8] The subject of the book

8. See A. Bartlett Giamatti, *Take Time for Paradise: Americans and Their Games,* 28–29. Giamatti discusses the Greek concepts of leisure and recreation, drawing upon Aristotle's ideas in *Nichomachean Ethics,* as cited by Michael O'Loughlin, *The Garlands Of Repose: The Literary Celebration of Civic and Retired Leisure,* 5–6.

would be *Sporting Lives,* an exploration of several key themes that are embedded in many athletes' stories, themes common in many ways to the larger culture but shaped by the way that sports make the world of the athlete a *particular* construction.

• From the Echoing Green to the End of Autumn

In writing the stories of their lives, the athlete has to make the subjective visible, to externalize the inner self in concrete ways, and the stages of life they select for special attention and the language they use to describe their experiences share strong similarities that I conceptualize in spatial and temporal terms. The arc of their narratives stretches from what I call the joyful expanses of "The Echoing Green" to the cold hillside of "The End of Autumn." Landscape as metaphor becomes a way of mapping the inner topography of the self. Athletes also externalize the self in the form of the body, which they paradoxically see as both self and dissociated object. And I argue that what animates the self and drives its external manifestations is a *genius loci,* a "spirit of place," a daimonic energy located in both the inner spirit and the body and expressed in sports performance. It is a form of imagination that the body makes visible. This special energy sometimes rises to the level of "magic," and it tracks the arc from "The Echoing Green" to "The End of Autumn" where it fades into the light of common day.

Describing the athlete's portrayal of his or her experiences on the playing field as an "Echoing Green," the subject of the first chapter, provides a way of understanding that many of these life stories present a cultural narrative that dramatizes sports as a rite of beautiful childhood. To conceptualize the athlete as an eternal child is to understand sports as a state of mind. Focusing closely on the language athletes use in their autobiographies, I argue in chapter 1 that they often construct from their subjective sense of daimonic energy an identity characterized by joy, playfulness, innocence, vitality, and spontaneity that corresponds to the "myth of origins" that we create for both our personal and historical pasts. Interpreting their experiences as those of a joyous child on an Edenic playing field reinforces the view that, as an autotelic ideal, sports is an "autotelic" activity, that is, a self-defined end or goal that the athlete refuses to bend to any external task, goal, or reward.

To be the eternal child, however, is to be cursed as well as blessed. This is the thesis of the second half of "The Echoing Green," and, taken together with the opening part of the chapter, is the first example of my argument that sports is a "Janus world."[9] If the echoing green is a bower of bliss, the implications of the bower are just as strong as those of the bliss. The world of sports is in certain key respects a sanctuary, a womblike pod that shelters and protects the athletes, but it also keeps them dependent. If childhood is the stage of life characterized by the most intensity of feeling, it is also the stage in which we have the least social power. The lives of athletes may often contain the magic of Peter Pan, but in very important ways athletes are more like Pan's companions, the "Lost Boys." During their playing careers they are "lost in the funhouse" of sports, running blind to many of the realities of the adult world from which their privileged status exempts them. This stage of the narrative of an athlete's life often becomes a period of prolonged infantilism characterized by an unhealthy dependence and sometimes leading to drug and alcohol abuse—all destructive consequences of their fixation on eternal youth. To live in the cloistered world of sports can mean delaying and frustrating another dimension of the self and, at worst, becoming trapped in the addictive and destructive mysteries of a cult.

Another distinctive construction of sports autobiographies is that they are in a significant sense "Body Songs." If the generic subject of all autobiographies is identity, I argue in the second chapter that, for athletes, the body is a crucial site of identity. The title of the classic feminist health book, *Our Bodies, Our Selves,* reverberates even more strongly for athletes because of their sense that the body *is* himself or herself. This view of self is not based upon privileging matter over mind but experiencing the self as it expresses itself through the body. Responding to the world as an "Echoing Green" is an imaginative act

9. Janus was the Roman god of gates and doorways, beginnings and endings. He was usually depicted with faces on both sides of his head, one looking in front and the other looking behind. In art criticism, a Janus symbol is one that symbolizes both one thing and its opposite at the same time. I use the concept to capture the contradictions and paradoxes in sports. Although he does not conceptualize sports as a Janus world, D. Stanley Eitzen's *Fair and Foul: Beyond the Myths and Paradoxes of Sport,* a sociological study of what he calls the "duality" of sports, its infectious play and its corruption as a spectacle and big business, provides a full treatment of what I call sports' Janus-like nature.

that athletes perform with the body. What some commentators call "physical genius" is another manifestation of the Greek concept of the daimonic, an energy or life force that also takes the form of sexuality and artistic creation.

Some of the most memorable "body songs" celebrate moments of what some athletes call "magic." A study of the language they use to describe these experiences, the subject of the third chapter, makes it clear that the term commonly used in kinesiology—"peak experience"—reduces to a physiological sensation what is much more complex. Athletes' accounts of these experiences portray them as something beyond the merely physical and temporal and suggest that they often rise to the level of what we might call the transcendent. The models for interpreting their descriptions of these experiences range from what cognitive psychologists call "chunking" to acts of imagination in which the athlete takes the vision in his or her head and makes it palpable with the body, and to mystical epiphanies that are almost beyond the reach of words or explanation.

Because the world of sports is a Janus world marked by opposing qualities and meanings, most athletes' "body songs" conclude on an elegiac note as the path from the "echoing green" leads to the "end of autumn." Athletes usually see their careers not as a drama marked by crescendo but as a kind of death. This final space on the narrative arc is the subject of the fourth chapter. Their autobiographical accounts reveal that they are most disturbed by the untimeliness of the coming "death." It is premature, an unnatural acceleration of the life cycle. The end of autumn suddenly darkens the echoing green, as if a season of their lives had somehow been elided.

Many sports autobiographies include confessions from athletes who at the end of their careers faced diminished lives and a diminished sense of self. In contrast to the echoing green's Edenic associations, life after sports is punctuated by a symbolic "fall." The "end of autumn" images in temporal form what the myth of the fall pictures spatially: an existence located outside the gates of Eden, which have closed forever. Most people mourn the passing of youth, but the athlete is the one who is most able to express his vision through the performance of the body, and the body has now betrayed him. The cultural significance of the athletes' "productions" of their lives is incomplete unless we understand the elegiac tone and the attempts to memorialize the self. It is necessary to see that the end of the arc represented by these autumnal reflections is determined by the privileging of its origins in "the echoing green."

To analyze athletes' subjective experiences of sports in the contemporary era also means considering that these experiences are shaped and altered by the ever-present, glaring eye of the media. Although many athletes continue to lay claim to some of the traditional narrative tropes of the American experience and to some of the seminal virtues defining American identity, the contemporary athlete is a celebrity. Like his predecessors, he usually insists upon the authenticity of his identity as a "self-made man," but the more telling tropes, images, and allusions in autobiographies argue the paradoxical thesis that the real self is synonymous with the "costumes" that reveal it. In the last chapter, I use Dennis Rodman—who has already written four autobiographies—as a case study for the contemporary athlete as postmodern celebrity. The postmodern self that emerges in Rodman's accounts is a fluid, protean self characterized by contradictions that make it an appropriate representation of the Janus world of sports.

Sports is so ingrained in the fabric of American life that few would dispute that it has become a valuable lens for understanding culture. Athletes' experiences become not just a mirror of culture but a magnifying glass. According to Neil Offen, one of the major attractions of sports is that it presents "life *in extremis;* every season you are born and you die; every 48 minutes or nine innings, you win and you lose. Every play encompasses an eternity."[10] *Sporting Lives* argues that the meaning of sports is intertwined with its narrativity, a thesis made more visible by focusing on the athletes' autobiographies, their own narratives of their lives in sports. Adding to the spotlight's power of magnification are the costumes, the rituals, and the intensity of the competition that turn the playing field or arena into a theater. Most athletes would claim that the drama of performance has the intensity to make that theater a place where the quotidian events of daily life are, as a poet once put it, "repeated in a finer tone."

This is the subjective view from inside the lines, but even those who disagree with this positive valuation can grant that sports is a

10. Neil Offen, *God Save the Players: The Funny, Crazy, Sometimes Violent World of Sports Fans,* xi.

world where many of the realities of culture are writ large. In the chapters that follow, my study of sports autobiographies is also a study of the celebration of youth and physical prowess, the search for magic in life, the nostalgia created by memories of things past, the desire to immortalize the self, and the growing awareness of mortality and last things that make sports an important window on the way we live now.

1

• • • • • • **"The Echoing Green"**

"Such such were the joys,
. . . On the Ecchoing Green."
~ *William Blake,* Songs of Innocence

"You gotta be a man to play baseball for a living, but
you gotta have a lot of little boy in you, too."
~ *Roy Campanella*

OUTSIDE MINUTE MAID PARK IN HOUSTON, TEXAS, MY hometown baseball stadium, are larger-than-life-size bronze statues of Craig Biggio and Jeff Bagwell. Both experts and fans agree that they are the two greatest players in the history of the Astros baseball team, but an important detail is that Biggio and Bagwell were still active players when the monuments were erected. A partial explanation for this speedy immortalization is that the history of the Houston franchise only goes back to 1962, and there were no other strong candidates for the iconography required to transform what would otherwise be only a business venue into a modern-day incarnation of the fans' desire for a "field of dreams."

Perhaps a similar logic explains why many people speak so readily of sports "heroes." Because the history of the country is so brief, many Americans find in sports the stuff of mythology that the older European countries locate in the mists of a distant past that was the haunt of those ancient giants who lived before the Flood. Babe Ruth became America's Beowulf, and the ballpark replicated the enclosed Garden of Eden so central to traditional lore. And if fans named Ruth "The Sultan of Swat" or, more recently, delighted in calling basketball star Charles Barkley "Sir Charles," the epithets are firm reminders that in America titles are not the entitlements of aristocratic birth or social class but awards for merit. According to the national myth, America's heroes are self-made individuals who rise to greatness in a democratic meritocracy, and sports is an expression of important cultural values because one of its virtues is that the rules are so clear and the competition so fair.

Despite current distractions such as labor conflicts between play-ers unions and the owners, controversies about testing for steroids and other performance-enhancing drugs, and increasing incidents of athletes being charged with domestic violence and other crimes, many people continue to idealize their favorite athletes. As the social problems involving legal and business issues, drugs, and violence make clear, their view of the athlete is grounded in something other than the daily news. Its source lies in a deeper need than mere facts can supply. Older fans' imaginations were shaped by the exploits of fictional athletes, such as Frank Merriwell and Dink Stover in the popular dime-novels and "books for boys" of the early twentieth cen-tury and the Chip Hilton series of novels published between 1948 and 1966. In recent years it is the Matt Christopher series of juvenile sports fiction books that have become best-sellers.[1]

Ken Garfield of the *Charlotte Observer* captured well the image that Clair Bee created in the twenty-three novels he wrote featuring Chip Hilton, as well as the hold they maintained on his memory:

> I can still see the Chip Hilton books lined up neatly in the bookcase of my bedroom, a collection more priceless than even baseball cards.

---

1. In the first part of his essay "House of Ruth, House of Robinson: Some Ob-servations on Baseball, Biography, and the American Myth" in *The Culture of Bruising: Essays on Prizefighting, Literature, and Modern American Culture,* Gerald Early discusses his boyhood reading of juvenile baseball biographies and their power of "narrativity," 131–37. He argues that these stories about the lives of the players provided him with a valuable orientation to the culture and that the books were "infinitely more interesting than watching the games themselves," 136.

To me and millions of other American boys growing up in the '60s, Chip was more than some slugger on TV who hit a home run in the bottom of the ninth to win the World Series. He was the straight-A, high school sports star who hit the homer, dated the homecoming queen and valued sportsmanship at all times.

He was a hero to kids with stars in their eyes. He was the guy we wished we could be. And even though he was fictional, he was as real as the hope we carried in our heart. Play fair, work hard and listen to your parents and you, too, could grow up to be as straight and tall and happy as Chip Hilton.[2]

The source of the description is also revealing. Garfield is not a sports columnist or a book reviewer but the *Observer*'s religion editor. The subject of the syndicated article is that the book series is being republished by Broadman and Holman, which Garfield identifies as a leader in the Christian book industry. He emphasizes the "strong spiritual backing" behind the new edition and reports that the project's organizer, VisionQuest of Dallas, is a sports marketing firm that "celebrates the positive side of sports." Garfield quotes a member of the organization who says he wants to "help fight the public perception that sports is only about money, trophies and Dennis Rodman." Garfield adds that even though the books are being modernized, "the core of the Chip Hilton series is unchanged."[3]

What Garfield admires is a vision of sports and the athlete that fans do not so much discover on the playing field or stadium as absorb from the larger culture, often in the form of books and movies like *The Pride of the Yankees* and *Knute Rockne All American* or, more recently, *Rudy* and *For Love of the Game*. The power of these cultural constructs and the feelings that underlie them is so strong that, as Garfield confesses about Chip Hilton, "even though he was fictional, he was as real as the hope we carried in our heart." In *Sport and the Spirit of Play in American Fiction,* Christian K. Messenger analyzes the way that American literature lionizes the athlete. Although he discusses fictional images of what he identifies as the Popular Hero and the School Hero, the purest ideal of the athlete, he argues, is found in literary figures he describes as examples of the Ritual Hero. While the Popular

2. Ken Garfield, "Chip Hilton Series Makes a Return."
3. Ibid.

Hero competes for immediate and tangible rewards such as money, fame, and records and the School Hero's aims are to win society's praise and to build the character that will prepare him for a leadership role in his community, the Ritual Hero participates in sports as an autotelic activity; unlike the Popular Hero and the School Hero, he does not engage in sports for utilitarian ends. For him, sports is about self-expression and self-fulfillment. It is its own reward.[4]

The cultural constructs at work in the fan's idealized conception of sports reach beyond his need for heroes, however. In fact, the success of movies like *Field of Dreams* points in another direction that has little to do with conceptions of heroes. The metaphor of the title reverberates with nostalgia, with the echoes of an imagined past that now resides only in memory. It is clear from Garfield's comments, and implicit in Messenger's analysis of sports literature, that many idealized views of sports and the athlete reflect a strong cultural bent toward nostalgia. What often binds the fan's days together are the memories of childhood and its pleasures, and sports is one of the strongest links he associates with that stage of his life.

This external view of sports is also reinforced by the athletes' own perspective from inside the lines, but, unlike the fan's memories, their nostalgia has some very specific implications that are unique to their experiences as participants for whom a childhood game has now become a career. A pervasive view in many autobiographies is that a strong part of the attraction that sports holds for them is its association with childhood. Whatever problems, trials, or crises they relate, most athletes celebrate their "love of the game." Central to their autobiographies is their testimony to their ability to keep alive feelings of pure joy that have their origin on the playgrounds of their youths. It is this state of mind and being that the poet William Blake describes in the lines, "While our sports shall be seen / On the Ecchoing Green."[5] Concepts like the green pastoral, the earthly paradise, and Eden represent cultural constructions that use spatial or geographical metaphors for this kind of psychological realm of innocence, playfulness, vitality, and spontaneity. These athletes' feel-

4. Christian K. Messenger, *Sport and the Spirit of Play in American Fiction: Hawthorne to Faulkner,* 8, 12, 231–32.

5. William Blake, *Selected Poetry and Prose of Blake,* 23. "The Ecchoing Green" is one of Blake's *Songs of Innocence.*

ings about sports are invested with nostalgia for what memory inscribes as a time in life when the imagination has not yet been fettered, a time when the child has not yet learned the objectivity that will sunder his realistic prospects from what Freud called "oceanic" intimations and possibilities. The echoing green of childhood sports that many athletes construct in their autobiographies is a landscape of desire, a "place" within the boy or girl at play where to desire is to have.

• The Eternal Child

If we can grant that, whatever its problems and harsh realities, sports has a mythic dimension for athletes as well as fans, then its power lies, like that of other myths, in its ability to re-create the sense of "the first time."[6] This sense does not take them back to the historical past, the dawn of creation. Instead, it recalls the joy they felt on the echoing green of their personal pasts. What Messenger defines as the Ritual Hero and what Bartlett Giamatti, Allen Guttmann, and other scholars explain more clinically as someone who engages in sports as an autotelic activity,[7] I conceptualize as the athlete's sense that he is the eternal child. For the athlete, to be a hero is in large part to keep alive the qualities of the child at play.

The media also reinforce this image of the athlete as a positive contrast to the portrait that emerges from the reports about off-the-field crimes and misdemeanors. The July 26, 1999, issue of *Sports Illustrated,* for example, featured a section on "The Century's Greatest Sports Photos" and an accompanying article on the least well-known of them, a locker room picture of the Texas Christian University football team before its 1957 Cotton Bowl match with the Jim Brown–led Syracuse University squad. At the end of the article there was another photograph that restaged the original picture with the men who were still alive forty-two years later. One of the most poignant

6. This phrase is Mircea Eliade's in *Rites and Symbols of Initiation: The Mysteries of Birth and Rebirth,* xiii.

7. See, for example, Giamatti, *Take Time for Paradise,* 14, and Allen Guttmann's books, *From Ritual to Record: The Nature of Modern Sports,* chapter 1, and *A Whole New Ball Game: An Interpretation of American Sports,* chapter 1.

parts of the article was the response to the old photo by one of the TCU players, Joe Williams:

> "You know something? Nothing ever again will match the intensity, the passion of moments like this. . . . Don't get me wrong, I love my wife and kids, but I'd give anything to go back. More than who you're looking at now, that guy in the picture, *that's* me. *That's* who I really am."[8]

The title of the article is "Moment of Truth," and the significance lies not only in the nostalgia Joe Williams feels but also in the authenticity and sense of identity he finds in the moment, that "first time," and the young man who having once been will be forevermore.

Such feelings reveal the workings of powerful cultural constructions. They have their origin not so much in what was as in what might have been. The French philosopher and novelist Jean-Jacques Rousseau once postulated that a crucial aspect of our understanding of self is based upon our creation of a myth of origins. The paradise we imagine is no more and, indeed, may never have been, but Rousseau argued that it is nevertheless necessary to have such a notion in order to interpret the diminished world in which we all live. Much of the cultural significance of sports is that, for the athlete and the fan, it brings back this "hour / Of splendour in the grass."[9]

The athlete feels, however, as if the gates around this Edenic past have not closed on him, that, unlike the fan, he still plays his sports on the echoing green. His conception of life assumes that this world of play is not a nostalgic dream of something that may have never been but a continuing reality. This is, at least in part, the state—the condition and the world—of the athlete as he or she describes it. And like most ambrosial gifts bestowed on mere mortals, it is both his blessing and his curse.

---

8. Gary Smith, "Moment of Truth," 138, 140.

9. Rousseau's idea appears in the "Preface" to his *Second Discourse,* as cited by Leslie Brisman, *Romantic Origins,* 11. In the "Preface" Rousseau "venture[s] some conjectures" about the difficulty of "separat[ing] what is original from what is artificial in the present state of man, and to know correctly a state which no longer exists, which perhaps never existed, which probably never will exist, and about which it is nevertheless necessary to have precise notions in order to judge our present state correctly." Jean-Jacques Rousseau, *The First and Second Discourses,* 92–93. William Wordsworth, *The Poetical Works of Wordsworth,* 355–56. The phrase is from "Ode: Intimations of Immortality from Recollections of Early Childhood."

If Pat Jordan's failure to reach the major leagues was "a false spring," then successful athletes live in a world in which the calendar's pages seem to remain stopped in a perpetual spring. The existence they construct is like the "green world" of Shakespeare's comedies and romances, a magical place where some of the normal rules of life are suspended. When Jordan reflects on the boys who left their homes to pursue careers as athletes, he thinks of that time in their lives as "the purest and the most precious dream they would ever have." In this green world, he explains, they experience "perpetual youth, innocence, the dream of playing a little boy's game for the rest of their lives. In their minds, no [other] dream would ever equal that." In *Ball Four* Jim Bouton makes the point bluntly: "Think of a ballplayer as a fifteen-year-old in a twenty-five-year-old body." America's fascination with sports rests in part on our recognition that the athlete is a kind of Peter Pan, an eternal child still playing games. Perhaps it is no coincidence that the greatest baseball player of all time was named "Babe" Ruth. Umpire Billy Evans's description of Ruth is probably typical of what his contemporaries thought of him: "Ruth is a big, likeable kid. He has been well named, Babe. Ruth has never grown up and probably never will. Success on the ball field has in no way changed him. Everybody likes him. You just can't help it."[10]

To say that the athlete is an eternal child is to understand sports as a state of mind. Bartlett Giamatti, the former professor of English and president of Yale University who later became commissioner of Major League Baseball, identifies with the athlete's idealistic perspective of his world when he writes about the significance of leisure as compared to work. Work is "a daily negotiation with death," he argues, but leisure is "the occasional transcendence of death." Leisure deserves this valuation because it is "a state of inner being which is, or is like, the freedom from care and obligation and travail."[11]

When we turn to athletes' accounts of what makes sports special, they do not portray themselves as heroes. Or rather, their construction of heroism is often not what traditional concepts of "sports heroes" would lead us to expect. Like Giamatti in his explanation of the

---

10. Jordan, *A False Spring*, 136. Jim Bouton and Leonard Shecter, *Ball Four*, 447. Evans is quoted by Benjamin G. Rader, "Compensatory Sport Heroes: Ruth, Grange and Dempsey," 12.
11. Giamatti, *Take Time for Paradise*, 22.

essence of sports, they often focus on a "state of inner being." State of being is a more accurate term than state of mind because the freedom play brings to the athlete flows from an inner wholeness that encompasses more than the mind or conscious thought. Like the child, the athlete at play is unself-conscious, totally absorbed in the moment. During the game he or she escapes the divorce between thought and feeling that is an all-too-common predicament of adult existence, particularly in our hurried, distracting society. This kind of primal wholeness the athlete describes feeling is not peaceful, however. It is dynamic and vital because the athlete sheds the layers between himself or herself and the daimonic spirit in the body. As I will explain in more detail in the chapter "Body Songs," the experience can be described as "thinking through the body."[12]

The athlete senses the presence of the daimonic in his response to it—in the deep power of joy he feels.[13] The point of view of Willie Mays's autobiography is that no athlete reveled in the joy of the game more than he did. It is significant that Mays has been immortalized as the "Say Hey Kid," another eternal child. The reviews cited inside his autobiography present its thesis as "the joy of baseball" and announce, "Willie Mays played out of love." Baseball to him was all in all. That is his interpretation of his life. Mays supports this image by recounting well-known stories about his fun playing stickball with the children in his neighborhood in New York during his early years with the Giants, and adds the interesting confession that on the road

12. The phrase is the title of Jane Gallop's book, *Thinking Through the Body*.

13. In Greek philosophy the daimon was a guardian spirit that guided man's destiny. Socrates referred to his daimon as a voice or sign which acted as a protective spirit: "My customary divination from the *daimonion* was always very frequent in all the former time, opposing me even in very small matters, if I were about to do something incorrectly." Thomas G. West, *Plato's Apology of Socrates: An Interpretation, with a New Translation*, 46. It is a spirit that serves as a link between the divine and the human. In all of its forms, this concept articulated the Greeks' ideas about the interrelationship between artistic creativity, religious zeal, the passion of love, rage, and madness. In modern psychology, scholars often take a different perspective, arguing that the daimonic can be a creative or a destructive force. They also discuss its darker side—rage, hatred, cruelty, and violence. See, for example, Rollo May, *Love and Will* (154–55, 158–59, 160, 161, 162, 163–64, 171–72). My use of the concept emphasizes its link to *genii* and thus to *genius*, a view that not only goes back to the positive sense in which Socrates used it in *The Apology* but also seems to be the way that poets, particularly visionary poets such as William Blake and William Butler Yeats, interpreted the concept.

he spent most of his time with Chris Durocher, the son of his manager, Leo Durocher. The seemingly uncomplicated story the autobiography presents is that of the selfless and unself-conscious love of a child for the game of baseball. The last two sentences of the autobiography end with a voice and point of view that sound like that of a child: "All I ever wanted was to play baseball forever. Leo always thought I could."[14]

Most great athletes testify to a similar feeling. Satchel Paige thought his older brother Wilson was a better player but that Wilson did not love baseball as much as he did. "You gotta LOVE it to play it good," he emphasizes in his autobiography, *Pitchin' Man*. "Me, I love it and live it." The meaning of this deep joy is suggested later in the autobiography when he refers to what he felt when he overcame a career-threatening arm injury as a "second childhood." When tennis great Bill Tilden talks about the athlete's "understanding of youth" and ability to ward off age by "keep[ing] the viewpoint of youth," however, it is more apparent that this aspect of the athlete's self-image is often a construction. The intensity of feeling causes most athletes to describe their joy as "pure" or "sheer." What they articulate is a freedom of spirit that reflects their ability to keep alive the child within themselves. Former Oakland Raider football player Chip Oliver's conversion to a radical view of politics and society during the late 1960s also transformed his approach to playing football. In *High for the Game* he relates that he suddenly realized, "Wow, this is child's play. . . . It was like playing in the streets as a kid again. I didn't care if I won or lost. All I wanted to do was play, just get it on and play. All this, I realized, . . . [was] the joy of playing football." Tennis player Pam Shriver explains in *Passing Shots* that, even with her chronically painful arm, she played because she "just had this all-consuming, little-kid kind of love for the game."[15]

Conceptualizing the athlete as a child carries along with it another defining quality, one that Jackie Robinson appropriates for himself in *I Never Had It Made* when he quotes a comment sports columnist Dick

14. Willie Mays and Lou Sahadi, *Say Hey: The Autobiography of Willie Mays*, 290.
15. Leroy Satchel Paige and Hal Lebovitz, *Pitchin' Man: Satchel Paige's Own Story*, 25, 59. William T. Tilden, 2nd, *My Story: A Champion's Memoirs*, 11–12. Chip Oliver and Ron Rapoport, *High for the Game*, 140. Pam Shriver, Frank Deford, and Susan B. Adams, *Passing Shots: Pam Shriver on Tour*, 16.

Young wrote about him. The often irascible Young, whom Robinson did not see as particularly sympathetic to him for most of his career, wrote that Robinson "has the tact of a child because he has the moral purity of a child."[16] The nature of this construction is striking when juxtaposed against news reports of increasing incidents of violence, drugs, and sexual abuse in sports. Equally revealing is the athlete's association of this purity and innocence with the child as opposed to the conventional scholarly view that these qualities are those of the adult Ritual Hero whose virtues are derived in the American tradition from Franklin and Emerson. The athlete tends to first locate his purity in the "pure" joy he feels in play.

Another aspect of the purity, however, is its autotelic distance from the corruption of money, which Franklin, on the other hand, viewed as the natural reward for virtue. In *A Running Tide,* for example, marathon runner Joan Benoit describes the purity of her motives: "I run because I love to—that's the way it's been from the beginning. If I stopped loving it I'd quit without a thought about the money."[17] It is tempting to dismiss her feelings as the luxury of an athlete competing in a sport with very limited commercial opportunities, particularly for women in the 1980s. But Bill Walton, who won basketball championships in both college and the NBA, entitles his autobiography *Nothing But Net* to symbolize his view of the purity of his love for the game, and he implies that professionals who play only for money are Judases who betray the game: "Some played for silver, I played for life." Because of his love for rock music he modifies the metaphor of the echoing green when he entitles one of the chapters of his autobiography "Strawberry Fields Forever." That state of being is where he was when he played the game. He compares his performance on the basketball court to a Grateful Dead concert, both of them driven by desire, the desire "to create, to build, to celebrate." He played in response to the daimonic spirit within him: "I needed the game. I craved it. I loved it. It was my passion." He is the eternal child, confessing, "all I ever wanted was more."[18] Whether the athlete is a professional or an amateur, a celebrity or an unknown, the point of view

16. Jackie Robinson and Alfred Duckett, *I Never Had It Made: An Autobiography,* 143.

17. Joan Benoit and Sally Baker, *Running Tide,* 141.

18. Walton and Wojciechowski, *Nothing But Net,* 6, 191, 6, 132.

and the construction are strikingly similar. They all testify, "Such, such were the joys on the echoing green."

In *A False Spring* Pat Jordan expresses a similar sentiment as he describes warming up for his tryout at Yankee Stadium:

> This moment, then, was what it was all about. My talent, after all, was simply a diversion. It existed as an end in itself, with no purpose beyond being perfected and enjoyed. Money, victories, strikeouts, batters even, were meaningless. . . . Nothing mattered but the simple act of throwing.[19]

The self-concept of athletes like Jordan is not a simple matter. They are not reducible to single labels like Ritual Hero or acquisitive celebrity. They are an interesting mix of motives, desires, and identities.

In the case of Jordan, however, he makes his claims about the purity of sports a seminal part of his construction of the process by which he lost it. He confesses he was greedy for a large bonus, and in his three years in the minors he at first clung to his identity as a "bonus baby"—the term used in Jordan's era of the 1950s for the relatively few baseball players who were given a signing bonus of as much as $50,000 to $100,000—to protect, in his own eyes as well as those of his teammates, a sense of self-worth that his performance did not warrant. Added to his willingness to subordinate his talent to his materialistic desires was a lack of the discipline and commitment to excellence that are central to the identity of the Ritual Hero. But he insists that a part of him knew he was most himself in the pure joy of throwing for the beauty of the act, and he later blamed his failure to make it to the majors not on a lack of talent, but on his corruption in compromising that talent for external reasons rather than ritualistically perfecting it. His quest for the largest bonus he could get was "the first time I had ever consciously used my talent, whose perfection had been my only end, as a means to another end."[20] This first temptation and failure led to the ultimate failure, fear of failure itself.

What marks his interpretation of his "false spring" as a version of "the echoing green" is that he associates his corruption, his "fall,"

---

19. Jordan, *A False Spring*, 41.
20. Ibid., 226–27.

with a loss of childhood. At the same time he was corrupting his natural "gift," his pitching arm, "like most adults," he confesses, "I was
learning to hide." He was now an Adam in shame, covering the signs
of his loss of innocence. The innocent in the garden had betrayed
himself. The child had vanished: "my talent . . . [was] the one thing
in me that was special to me. It doesn't matter what that thing was. . . .
It only matters that such a thing did exist in me, as it does in us all,
and that by refusing to risk perfecting it I was denying what most
truly defined me."[21]

Another sign that this is a construction is encoded in the later trajectory of Jordan's life. The reflection required to write his autobiography led him to an awareness that his character flaws included an
unfeeling distance from other people. After his first sexual experience with a young, small-town Nebraska girl in the backseat of an automobile at a drive-in movie theater, he sarcastically asked her, "Did
anything move?" Fourteen years later he was to discover that he was
the father of her child and that, contrary to his harsh assumptions
about her, she had not tried to entrap him to escape from a bleak future but thought of their brief relationship as one of the most exciting
periods of her life that she remembers only fondly. When he identifies the defect in his character as not getting along with his teammates and rejecting the kind overtures of the people with whom he
boarded, he admits that in writing about these people, "[I] lend to
myself a sensitivity on paper I lack in reality."[22] The negative self-
judgment doesn't become the real point. By the time he writes *A False
Spring* Jordan has become a successful freelance journalist for *Sports
Illustrated, Esquire,* and other major periodicals, and the implicit irony
is that the very distance that made him a flawed human being is inseparable from the aesthetic detachment that is one of the essential
aspects of his success as a writer.

• Sports and the Myth of Origins

What are we to make, then, of the view that these athletes present of
themselves as the eternal child in an Edenic echoing green? Clearly,

21. Ibid., 232, 227.
22. Ibid., 110, 156.

it is a cultural construction that reflects our fixation with youth and beauty. Patricia Meyer Spacks, a scholar of eighteenth-century British literature, has written about the significance of the particular life stage that a culture privileges. She argues that the eighteenth century, for example, valued full maturity so highly that many autobiographers in effect "denied their childhoods," condensing that part of their lives into a few anecdotes.[23] Some athletes give only brief accounts of their childhoods in their autobiographies, choosing, like the eighteenth-century writer, to focus on what they have done rather than on what they have felt or who they are. I suspect, however, that their lack of attention to their early life usually has less to do with cultural values than with the general lack of quality of these autobiographies. They are chronicles of facts and events that seem to have very limited contributions from the athlete.

Spacks argues that adolescence is the life stage that receives the most attention in twentieth-century autobiographies, its attraction centered on its association with defiance and difference, and that childhood is the dominant subject in nineteenth-century autobiographies. This schema suggests additional implications about the prominence of "the echoing green" in sports autobiographies. Choosing childhood as a key structure for conceptualizing their experiences and identity reveals the romantic nature of the way these athletes cast their life stories. Long before Freud, romantic writers such as Rousseau and Wordsworth celebrated childhood. When Wordsworth wrote, "The Child is father of the Man," his conception of the relationship between the past and the present, between childhood and the self the adult creates, was very different from Freud's ideas about the effect of early psychic traumas on human development.[24] For him, the focus on the personal past provided a way of writing a "myth of origins" and idealizing the child for his naturalness and imaginative grasp of experience and the world. The Romantic era was the dawn of modernity and announced the centrality of the self and the subjective. It asserted

23. Patricia Meyer Spacks, "Stages of Self: Notes on Autobiography and the Life Cycle," 46.
24. Wordsworth, *The Poetical Works of Wordsworth*, 277. This is the first line of a poem titled, "My Heart Leaps Up When I Behold," and Wordsworth later used the phrase as an epigram for his poem, "Ode: Intimations of Immortality from Recollections of Early Childhood."

the value of the feelings—of spontaneity, of "that primal joy which having been must ever be,"[25] that is, of the daimonic and the other qualities that we have seen athletes claim as the source of their identity, their "birth" right. Even those iconoclastic athletes whom we might expect to emphasize adolescence and its rebellion—writers of exposés such as Jim Bouton and Dave Meggysey—identify themselves as purists who attack the corrupt forces that have robbed the game they love of its innocence. Their point of view still reflects its origin on "the echoing green."

But as Rousseau pointed out, a "myth of origins," whether that construction of the past ever actually existed or not, derives its meaning not from the past but from the present. It is a fiction, not in the sense that it is false, but in the sense that it is a story, a construct, that explains what cannot be explained in a more rational or logical way, and its purpose is to provide a perspective on the present situation that we face. It is, therefore, a necessary fiction. It expresses a nostalgic longing that perforce intimates a problematic current condition. Many athletes come to understand that to be the eternal child is to be cursed as well as blessed.

• "The Lost Boys"

If the echoing green is a bower of bliss, the implications of the bower are just as strong as those of the bliss. The world of sports is in certain key respects a sanctuary, a womblike pod that shelters and protects the athletes but also keeps them dependent. We often think of athletes more than of most other people as "pampered," and the epithet points to our conception of them as children who rely upon the care of others, as well as to our recognition of the privileged status which the culture grants them. The athlete may be the eternal child, but we must remember that childhood is both the stage of life characterized by the most intensity of feeling and the stage in which we have the least social power. There is a crucial distinction between playing a sport with such joy that it keeps alive the child within and being pampered so that we never grow up. The lives of athletes testify to the rel-

25. Ibid., 356.

evance of both conceptions of them. Their lives contain the magic of Peter Pan, but in a very important way they are more like Pan's companions, the "Lost Boys." During their playing careers they are "lost in the funhouse" of sports, running blind to many of the realities of the adult world from which their privileged status exempts them.

In *Life on the Run* Bill Bradley frames his diary with an introductory passage from F. Scott Fitzgerald's essay "Ring":

> During those years, when most men of promise achieve an adult education, if only in the school of war, Ring moved in the company of a few dozen [men] . . . playing a boy's game. A boy's game, with no more possibility in it than a boy could master, a game bounded by walls which kept out novelty or danger, change or adventure. . . .[26]

With this image we encounter one of the many troubling paradoxes of sports. Sports' sanctuary walls in; it walls out. It cloisters these privileged elect; it protects these pampered children from both problems and routine hassles. The source of this condition of prolonged infantilism lies neither solely in the athlete nor in the attitudes of others but in their interrelationship. Like a child, the athlete demands the care of others, but his treatment by parents, coaches, and adoring fans has conditioned him to expect that care. The result, as *New York Times* writer and book author John Lipsyte breezily expresses it, is that in American culture athletes are "waved, as it were, through the tollbooths of life."[27]

Their dependence and the ultimately harmful "nurturing" athletes receive appear most clearly in the way they characterize their relationships with their coaches. Many sports autobiographies follow the pattern of the bildungsroman, the story of a quest for identity that takes place as part of an initiation into the larger social world. They often include the corollary motif of the search for the father, a role often played in the case of the athlete by his coaches. An important subject in *Say Hey* is Willie Mays's relationship with his first major-league manager, Leo Durocher. Mays, a black athlete playing only five years after Jackie Robinson integrated major-league baseball, freely admits he found a father figure in Durocher, who was white,

26. Bill Bradley, *Life on the Run*, 2.
27. John Lipsyte, "Varsity Syndrome: The Unkindest Cut," 116.

but the pattern began earlier when he was in the minor leagues. His first manager, Chick Genovese, watched over him and sat and ate with him in the kitchen when restaurants refused to serve blacks in the dining room. Their talks, Mays remembers, "were moments I still treasure."[28] His next manager, Tommy Heath, was also protective, and when Mays was called up to the New York Giants he at first refused to go because he was afraid. His fears reflect the double-edged nature of the sanctuary. Mays believed he needed a father figure to care for him, particularly because of the racism he faced in the minors, but the care also made him overly dependent and blocked his emotional growth. The pattern was repeated when he reached the majors, and Mays's account reveals the destructive problems underlying being a man who professes a child's selfless and unself-conscious "love" for the game.

The dark undersong of the "Say Hey Kid" registers an oblivion to care, obligation, and other demands of the adult world. Mays recognized that Durocher spoke to him "in that fatherly way" that he did not use with the other players and that he "loved me."[29] Durocher also assigned an older black player, Monte Irvin, to look after Mays his rookie season and later sent him money and continued to father him even when Mays was in the army. As much as Mays may think he needed this paternalism, it also stunted him in important ways. He bought a car with his first paycheck, but he did not know how to drive it and so a friend had to chauffeur him. Even though he was one of the highest-paid players in 1962, more than a decade after he became a major-leaguer, he was chronically broke and had to borrow against his salary. In these and other similar confessions, Mays's autobiography reveals the interplay between the general culture of sports and the more specific historical context of the black experience in the 1950s and 1960s, particularly the destructive form of indentured servitude that was common in the South for almost a hundred years after the end of slavery.

Mays's dilemma is that he remained the "Say Hey Kid" even after he retired from baseball. "Now here I was forty-three years old," he realized, "and I still was expecting people to make decisions for me." He had always taken great pride that he "played out of love," but in

28. Mays and Sahadi, *Say Hey,* 45.
29. Ibid., 65, 76.

his speech when he was inducted into the Baseball Hall of Fame he confessed, "I sacrificed a bad marriage and I sacrificed a good marriage. But I'm here today because baseball is my number one love."[30] "Sacrifice" is a telling choice of words. It reveals the self-centeredness of a child who doesn't think of the consequences for the women in his life as even collateral damage. The autobiography's undeveloped reference to the two failed marriages also undercuts the seeming simplicity of the main narrative the autobiography presents of Mays as the man-child.

The paternal structure of the sports culture molded the self-images of many white players as well. In *Instant Replay*, his diary about a championship season with the Green Bay Packers, Jerry Kramer says proudly about Coach Lombardi's view of him and his teammates, "His players are his children," and he writes the book with the presence of Lombardi, whom he is absolutely devoted to pleasing, always falling across his shoulder. Boxer Jack Dempsey recounts in his autobiography a vacation he took in Paris without his manager, Doc Kearns, along. He sounds like a child when he excitedly describes the unaccustomed freedom he felt: "For once there was no Doc or anyone else to tell me what to eat and drink or how to act." The problem is not Kearns personally but the culture that directs the athlete and keeps him an eternal child. Switching managers did not change the nature of Dempsey's dependence, for he relates later in the book that his new manager, Leo Flynn, "told me what to do from the moment I got up till my head hit the pillow at night."[31]

Sports was also an echoing green for Dave Meggysey, an escape from the drunken father who physically abused him and the feelings of inferiority that were the lot of the children of immigrants like him. In *Out of Their League*, he writes about his realization that, as long as he played football, he was a child in his search for surrogate fathers in the coaches he desperately wanted to please and in the purity of his refusal to yield to under-the-table money when he was in college or other corruptions that belied the joy of playing for its own sake. Unlike Chip Oliver's experiences, however, his conversion by the radical politics of the 1960s did not transform his view of the game in

30. Ibid., 273, 274.
31. Kramer and Shaap, *Instant Replay*, 50. Jack Dempsey and Barbara Piattelli Dempsey, *Dempsey*, 149, 211.

a positive way. Instead, it only made him aware of the utilitarian ends that even he was vulnerable to. He retired because he "just [couldn't] separate the game from the payoffs—approval, money, adulation."[32] The loss of innocence may be inevitable, but it only underscores the power of the echoing green while it lasts.

The passivity and dependence fostered by the coach are mirrored almost everywhere else in the athlete's life. In *Ball Four* Jim Bouton explains, "Being a professional athlete allows you to postpone your adulthood. You grow up in Heroworld. Parents change the dinner schedule for you, teachers help with grades, coaches fawn over you, cops ask for an autograph and someone else buys the drinks. Or worse." He then quotes Bill Russell: "most professional athletes have been on scholarship since the third grade." In *Throwing Heat* and *I Had a Hammer* both Nolan Ryan and Hank Aaron comment on baseball players' lack of self-sufficiency. They have no need to develop this trait of maturity because day-to-day details are taken care of by business managers, clubhouse managers, and traveling secretaries. In *Beyond Center Court* tennis player Tracy Austin confesses, "I have never paid a bill; I've always had financial advisers do it for me."[33]

As wonderful as this may sound to some people, it reflects an unnatural seclusion from the realities of the larger social world. Those who live privileged lives are special, but the sort of situation and the context described in these accounts have clear negative implications. As Austin admits, she "basically lived a rather selfish life. This is not unusual. This is typical behavior for all the top athletes I know."[34] When she explains her comment by pointing out that she needed ten hours of sleep at night, the image is not that of a privileged hero but a pampered child.

The selfishness she confesses to is a product of the special dispensation the culture grants to athletes. In *Violent Sundays*, former football player Bob Chandler writes that when he was at the University of Southern California the football players expected to have "gofors" register for them, and they parked illegally in restricted zones because they knew the tickets would be fixed for them. Fifteen years

32. Dave Meggysey, *Out of Their League*, 65.
33. Bouton and Shecter, *Ball Four*, 447. Tracy Austin and Christine Brennan, *Beyond Center Court: My Story*, 210.
34. Austin and Brennan, *Beyond Center Court*, 125.

after the publication of Chandler's autobiography the newspapers were reporting that football players at crosstown rival UCLA were routinely parking in handicapped parking spaces on campus with no repercussions. When Lawrence Taylor writes in his autobiography, *LT: Living on the Edge*, about how North Carolina football coach Bill Dooley was "into looking after his players," the example he cites is that Dooley made sure they "weren't going to get too hassled with their courses or with the university administration."[35]

Not all athletes respond to this sense of entitlement and immunity by committing crimes as some Oklahoma football players, for example, did during the lawless era at that university in the late 1970s and early 1980s, but many do act in accord with the unhealthy treatment they come to expect and demand. Jerry West, the "All-American Boy" who starred for the Los Angeles Lakers, complains that "Pro athletes are the most spoiled people in the world," and a prime example was West's peer, Rick Barry. In *Confessions of a Basketball Gypsy*, Barry admits, "I'm like a boy, sometimes. I've tried to control myself [his temper, his practice of taunting other players], but I can't." Babe Ruth was far more likable than Barry and escaped his reputation for petulance, but in his autobiography when he stands back and reflects upon one of his many escapades he realizes he "had acted like a spoiled child." And Ted Williams acknowledges that his "war against the world" was not based upon principle. Williams's obscene gestures and episodes of spitting at the fans were the childish displays of someone who admits that he was "prone to tantrums."[36] These recurring examples make it clear that being an eternal child, whatever its positive implications, is also a sign of a serious problem that is endemic to the world of sports.

Football players John Brodie in *Open Field* (a different sort of sports autobiography in the sense that he presents his life as flawed by a problem whose answer he ultimately finds in Scientology) and Lance Rentzel in *When All the Laughter Died in Sorrow* (an equally off-beat life story of a "golden boy" married to a Hollywood starlet but driven to expose himself to children) both use the recurring metaphor of

35. Lawrence Taylor and David Falkner, *LT: Living on the Edge*, 52.
36. Jerry West and Bill Libby, *Mr. Clutch: The Jerry West Story*, 152. Rick Barry and Bill Libby, *Confessions of a Basketball Gypsy: The Rick Barry Story*, 77. Babe Ruth and Bob Considine, *The Babe Ruth Story*, 139. Ted Williams and John Underwood, *My Turn at Bat: The Story of My Life*, 79.

the "security blanket" to describe the insulating nature of the sports sanctuary, but another of the dangers of this sheltered life is that it often fosters, in addition to dependence, the athlete's childlike belief in his or her freedom from consequences and responsibilities. When Bob Chandler played for the Buffalo Bills his wife, Marilyn, stayed in their California apartment during the football season, and Chandler realized that he liked the life of a "married bachelor" with no responsibilities. It was perfectly consistent with the mentality of a football player living in a world free of adult cares. Even a person of unusual character like Rosey Grier, perhaps better known as the friend and bodyguard of Bobby Kennedy during his quest for the presidency than as a former outstanding tackle in the National Football League, confesses in his autobiography that he was a "reluctant groom" when he married. He wanted intimacy but "nothing to do with being a husband and father" who would be "shackled with responsibility."[37] In *Rosey: The Gentle Giant,* he blames football for encouraging him to indulge his desire to play the role of a child, and confesses he preferred that role to being an adult father and husband.

One of the sports autobiographies that most explicitly conceptualizes the athlete's life as a destructive perpetual childhood is John Lucas's *Winning a Day at a Time.* When Lucas says he "led a special life," he has in mind more than his talent in basketball and tennis. It was not just that "everything was taken care of for me." He was also exempt from doing any chores at home. He learned very young to read the many signs that implied athletes like him did not have to accept responsibility. If he grew accustomed to the comfort of sports as "a very safe, sheltered environment," he later saw that, from another perspective, it was "a tight structure" that walled him off from much of life and denied him the freedom he needed to experiment in his search to discover who he was.[38] Because he lacked a normal breadth of experience, his only strategy for learning was to take athletic principles and apply them to general life.

This proved to be woefully inadequate. It created a distorted view of reality because, as he observes, "I had become an adult in sports,

---

37. Bob Chandler and Norm Chandler Fox, *Violent Sundays,* 95. Roosevelt "Rosey" Grier and Dennis Baker, *Rosey: The Gentle Giant,* 137.
38. John Lucas and Joseph Moriarity, *Winning a Day at a Time,* 29, 89, 42.

but I was still a child in the rest of life." By the time he reached the pros, "Basketball and tennis had become who I was rather than what I did. I didn't know who I was." This self-analysis was the product of many years of digging for the reasons for the destructive behavior that was caused by his arrested development. The most dramatic problem was his chronic drug abuse, which froze him in time as "a little lost child." This is a recurring image in his autobiography. His recovery was a slow, painful process. His colleagues in the hospital corporation where he was employed in the area of drug rehabilita- tion described their initial efforts in working with him as like "rais- ing a son," and he compares the efforts of his friends who helped him to return to the NBA as "like . . . getting their son ready for the prom." In his case, Alcoholics Anonymous's twelve-step program offered the support he needed to become the person he wanted to be. "When I got sober," he writes, "I grew up."[39] Peter Pan is a wonderful icon of the magic of childhood, but, as John Lucas came to understand, the danger is becoming one of the "Lost Boys," bewildered by the sober- ing disenchantments of adulthood that inevitably intrude upon the athlete's sheltering but fragile sanctum.

- ## Sports as a Cult

Lucas's drug addiction has some additional implications. While it may be true that the incidences of drug abuse by athletes are not dis- proportionate to those of the larger population, the contributing fac- tors in their cases may have some relationship to the culture of sports. Historians have discovered that sport has its origins in religious fer- tility rituals, and even modern-day sport retains something of the cul- ture of a cult, a world set apart. Like initiates in a cult, athletes are persons of privilege because of their extraordinary bodies and their mastery of the physical arts. Nonathletes are excluded from the cult, but not just because they lack the necessary physical skills. They also lack the state of mind and the identity that are essential to member- ship in the cult. They have their own versions of the echoing green, their experiences of release and freedom, but they understand the

39. Ibid., 66, 77, 105, 114, 117.

deep chasm that divides this realm from the quotidian world of work
and care. The tendency of some athletes is to lose sight of that dividing chasm, or perhaps not to recognize its existence. When this is the
case, the athlete becomes totally devoted to and absorbed in sports.
The reasons are not hard to understand. He is told he is special and
treated with an admiration or reverence that youth does not deserve,
is not prepared for, and cannot adequately handle. There is also the
single-minded focus, the obsession almost, that is necessary if one is
to be a great athlete—all the hours of practice and training, the tunnel
vision that segregates him from other activities and interaction with a
wide variety of nonathletes. It is significant that Jack Nicklaus attributes much of his greatness as a golfer to what he frequently refers to
in his autobiography as a "cocoon of concentration."[40] The problem is
that some athletes spin this cocoon around their whole lives.

What we see again is that sports is a state of mind, and that the
sanctuary it creates is more psychological than literal. Despite the
reputation that college athletes have as beer drinkers and bullies who
take out their aggression on women and nerds, alcohol abuse, sex-
ism, and antisocial belligerence cut across the various college campus
groups and are hardly the exclusive sins of athletes. What is really
distinctive of college athletes is the way that their culture segregates
them from the mainstream of college life. First of all, the hours their
sport demands make it the equivalent of a full-time job. Second, although they are expected to stay eligible, college athletes are usually
not encouraged to participate in the full intellectual life of the college. Many athletes choose respectable majors, but the athlete with
the potential to play professional sports is likely to major in the traditional field of physical education or relatively recently created majors such as sports management or sports administration. It is also
very common, perhaps even standard in many universities, for one
of the coaches to register for the athlete, telephone the adviser about
his performance in his courses, and speak to the instructor about
problems that arise. The effect of this paternalism is that the coach
rather than the athlete negotiates between the world of sports and the
academic world, reinforcing the athlete's isolation and thus his ab-
sorption in the cult. Some people are surprised at how articulate
many former athletes are when they become sports broadcasters, but

40. Jack Nicklaus and Ken Bowden, *Jack Nicklaus: My Story*, 34, 59, 90.

what they fail to consider is that, as a cult, sports has a lore and customs of its own, and the athlete who has devoted his life to the cult to the exclusion of all else is adept in its mysteries, if not in what remains for him the unexplored world of Shakespeare, Heisenberg, and other academic subjects.

In his ideas about the relationship between Americans and their games, Bartlett Giamatti defines a cult as the mindscape that we inhabit when "we veer into the special world of a sport in order to live there, rather than to visit."[41] It is the former that is the fate and condition of the "Lost Boys." Giamatti also points out that drugs or alcohol can take on a special significance in the cult of sports. They become a way for the elite initiates to affirm their membership in the closed culture and to convey their sense of their specialness. This behavior is very similar to that found in the Greek culture on college campuses, and it is interesting that Reggie Jackson says that playing with the Oakland A's "was the college experience I'd never had" and that the locker room was "like a college frat house."[42] Athletes often comment on the adrenaline "rush" they feel in the heat of competition, and runners such as Lynda Huey refer to their "addiction" to the physical pleasures of their sport. Drugs and alcohol re-create this feeling for some athletes. That is why Chip Oliver entitles his autobiography *High for the Game*. But, as Giamatti implies, the drugs also reinforce the nature of the cult. Psychologically, they help the athlete to absorb himself in the cult and leave behind reminders of the world of work, obligations, and worries. Those athletes whose cloister includes a heightening haze of drugs become like Tennyson's "Lotos-Eaters" in the poem of that name. They eat the fragrant blossoms of the lotus to remain on an island far from home, where it is always afternoon.

• Where Life Is "Repeated in a Finer Tone"

Conceptualizing sports as an echoing green filled with eternal children adds another dimension to its political, social, and cultural meaning. The image ties sports once again to the national myth. It

41. Giamatti, *Take Time for Paradise*, 56. For Giamatti's discussion of sports as a cult, see 56–59.
42. Reggie Jackson and Mike Lupica, *Reggie: The Autobiography*, 86, 188.

represents the freedom that the first English settlers sought. It also symbolizes the fountain of youth that Ponce de Leon hoped to find in the New World. In his book on sports, literature, and culture Gerald Early argues that, as a cultural image, baseball does not remind us of childhood "so much as it *transfixes* it." While sports mirrors the cultural obsession with youth, the athletes' accounts and constructions of their experiences reveal a more inclusive and complex rendering of this aspect of American culture. To live in the echoing green's cloistered world is to keep alive much of the best of the child within each person. To attempt to remain in its sheltering enclosure, however, is to delay and frustrate other dimensions of the self and, at worst, to become lost in the addictive and destructive mysteries of a cult. The problem is that even the self-aware athlete believes that the dangers of the latter cannot approach the joys and pleasures of the former. Bill Bradley speaks for many athletes when he quotes Fitzgerald's essay "Ring": "It was never that he was completely sold on athletic virtuosity as the be-all and end-all of problems; the trouble was that he could find nothing finer." What compounds the problem for the athlete is that he, like Ring, believes that the enclosed garden that is sports is a place where, as Keats wrote in one of his letters, "what we call happiness on Earth [is] repeated in a finer tone."[43]

Many of today's fans grouse that the ills of sports exist because the game is hardly "all-consuming" for most players. They scorn the extent to which the modern player is a greedy opportunist who is overpaid by any reasonable standard and more concerned about the performance of his investment portfolio than his team's record. While it is true that the era of sports as big business and the athlete as celebrity has changed the game, it is a mistake, I think, to assume that many if not most modern athletes haven't maintained the childlike joy for the game that the old-timers boast about. The myth of generations past is misleading. According to Grantland Rice, one of the great sportswriters during the "Golden Age of Sports," Babe Ruth was the first athlete to be sold to the public as much for his color, personality, and crowd appeal as for his athletic ability,[44] and Ty Cobb, for all his railings

43. Early, *The Culture of Bruising*, 138. Bradley, *Life on the Run*, 2. John Keats, *Complete Poems and Selected Letters of John Keats*, 489. The phrase appears in Keats's November 22, 1817, letter to Benjamin Bailey.
44. As cited by Christopher Lasch, "The Corruption of Sports," 63.

against what later ballplayers were doing to his beloved game, was a preeminent capitalist who was the first player to become a millionaire based upon his salary and the investments he made with it. On the other side of the generational divide, Pete Rose reflects the same cultural complexities. His ruling image is "Charlie Hustle," a "throwback" player who epitomized the purity of the game as it was played by the old-timers. As sports historian Richard C. Crepeau describes him and other modern-day Horatio Algers, they are "old myths in new models."[45] In addition to the scandals about his sports betting, however, Pete Rose is also a model of the athlete as consumption idol, hawking himself everywhere from meetings of card collectors to television commercials for hair cream and various promotional activities. He even showed up one year in Cooperstown selling bats and other memorabilia outside the hallowed grounds of the Baseball Hall of Fame from which he has been excluded. The athletes' accounts in their autobiographies imply that being a celebrity or becoming a multimillionaire businessman does not mean that they can't still see themselves as the eternal child playing for the love of the game. As Joe Frazier, a boxer who lacked the charisma of his nemesis Muhammad Ali and never became much of a celebrity or a really rich man, said about himself, boxing "wasn't just a job to me. It was my pleasure and passion."[46] The reality isn't one or the other but a simultaneous juxtaposition of seeming opposites.

45. Richard C. Crepeau, "Sport, Heroes and Myth," 30.
46. Joe Frazier and Phil Berger, *Smokin' Joe: The Autobiography of a Heavyweight Champion of the World, Smokin' Joe Frazier*, 123.

2

• • • • • • • • • •   **Body Songs**

All thoughts and actions emanate from the body. Every idea,
intuitive or intellectual, can be imaged and translated in terms of
the body, its flesh, blood, sinews, veins, glands, organs, cells, or
senses.

~ *Dylan Thomas*

When I was little, I was big.

~ *William "The Refrigerator" Perry*

ROGER J. PORTER OBSERVES THAT MOST AUTOBIOGRAPHIES
do not focus on the body because the authors assume that their
physical being is neither sufficiently distinctive nor interesting. Porter argues, however, that the body sometimes becomes a
locus for autobiographical investigations into the psyche. To under-
score his point, he quotes a French feminist, Chantal Chawaf: "Isn't
the final goal of writing to articulate the body? . . . The word must
comfort the body . . . reconnect the book with the body."[1]

Sports autobiographies may seem to be a world far distant from
that which French feminists find attractive to study, but it is hardly

---

1. Roger J. Porter, "Figuration and Disfigurement: Herculine Barbin and the
Autobiography of the Body," 122. He quotes Chawaf's "Linguistic Flesh," translated by Yvonne Rochette-Ozzello, in Elaine Marks and Isabelle de Courtivron,
eds., *New French Feminisms: An Anthology*, 177–78.

surprising that athletes would find their bodies to be distinctive and interesting. The explicit stories athletes tell may be Horatio Alger rags-to-riches tales in which they rise from the slum or the rural province to fame and fortune on the athletic field or court, but the implicit story often involves reading their bodies as if they were texts. Athletes' views of their identities that they recount and explore in their autobiographies have their origins in both the social world in which they live and the more intimately known bodies which they inhabit.

• Our Bodies: Our Selves

To understand that much of the athlete's subjective sense of self has its origins in the body, we begin with the obvious fact that sports, un-like games such as chess, are physical activities, and that the authors of sports autobiographies are athletes who usually have extraordinary bodies. In the present era offensive linemen in pro football routinely weigh well above three hundred pounds and many basketball players are literally giants. While baseball players tend to occupy a more human scale, even in high school the hitters with the most promise characteristically have noticeably strong bodies that easily identify them as the "son of the village blacksmith" type. The bodies of great athletes are extraordinary in quality as well as quantity. They are not just larger but sculpted. Our greater knowledge about nutrition and the use of sophisticated weight training are partially responsible. So are the increasing organization and professionalization of sports, which result in intensive physical cultivation of young athletes of promise. For the average person, the body becomes almost a buried part of the self after childhood, but for great athletes the body remains often the most essential part of who they are. We all construct identities, but the athlete constructs an identity through his or her body.

Because most people privilege mind over matter, they forget what they once knew about themselves as children—the sense of physical vitality that the poet Wordsworth describes as "glad animal movements." They forget that the imagination is only one expression of an energy or life force that also has a physical manifestation. It is what the Greek philosophers sometimes referred to as the daimonic, a powerful spirit or drive within people that they later came to fear

and identify with the demonic as they cultivated the arts of civiliza-
tion. The nonathlete recognizes this energy for what it truly is only as
it appears in artistic creation and sexuality. In *Ball Four,* former baseball player, sportscaster, and actor Jim Bouton gets at this essence of
sports when he divides athletes into three categories: those who do
everything instinctively, those who are intelligent, and those who are
intelligent enough to know that baseball is basically an instinctive
game. In his autobiography *Out of Bounds* Jim Brown, the Hall of
Fame running back for the Cleveland Browns, is more direct: "bottom line, man is a physical being."[2]

NFL Films began the glamorization of pro football with a dramatic
heightening of its violence featuring slow-motion replays, soaring
music soundtracks, and amplified sounds of bodily collisions. Some
admirers tout football as a reminder of the animalistic violence that
is a part of human nature, a literal "rage against the darkness" that
belies our illusions about the extent of human evolution. That view
takes in only a small part of the daimonic, however. This energy is a
life force, but in most sports its realization has more to do with life
rather than with force. Sports engage the athlete with the physical
rhythm of life in a visceral way. They awaken—or keep alive—a
sense of self that is as basic as the body's pulse or the recurring beats
of the blood's diastolic and systolic movements. Jim Brown describes
the sensation of running as an experience in which his senses were
"ridiculously heightened" and adds, "Physically, I don't know that
I've ever felt more alive." The athlete lives in a world where the body
and the senses are the center of his existence. In his autobiography
Outrageous! basketball player Charles Barkley argues that athletes
"know our bodies better than most people know their families," and
for all his posing and the confusions in his life former NBA player
Dennis Rodman claims with certainty: "I know my body." And in his
autobiography *Yaz,* Carl Yastrzemski, the former Boston Red Sox
baseball player, echoes what most athletes believe: "One thing I
knew, and that was my body."[3]

2. Wordsworth, *The Poetical Works of Wordsworth,* 92. The phrase is from "Tintern Abbey." Bouton and Shecter, *Ball Four,* 22. Jim Brown and Steve Delsohn, *Out
of Bounds,* 148.

3. Brown and Delsohn, *Out of Bounds,* 113. Barkley and Johnson, *Outrageous!*
272. Dennis Rodman and Tim Keown, *Bad as I Wanna Be,* 253. Carl Yastrzemski
and Gerald Eskenazi, *Yaz: Baseball, the Wall, and Me,* 212.

• **"Wildness": The Body as Dilated Self**

The implicit theme of many sports autobiographies is that knowing the body is a way of knowing the self. In his reflections on football in *The End of Autumn* Michael Oriard says that when he first played the game, it gave him a confidence and strength that was clear and simple at a time when the rest of his adolescent life was filled with awkwardness and uncertainty. It was a provisional identity until he could create a second identity that would take into account the complexities of the larger social world. He conceptualizes the sense of self that emanated from his body as a primal identity, a fusion with life that needed nothing else to complete itself:

> As a football player my body was a barometer that registered all the sensations created by my surrounding environment. I was acutely aware of sun, rain, stiff winds, light breezes, dryness, humidity, grass, mud, the dirt of skinned infields, when we played in baseball stadiums—even snow and sleet on rare occasions. All of it *alive*. All of it making *me* feel more intensely alive.[4]

It is clear from his description that, for Oriard, the life of the body is not a lesser life. In fact, in many ways it is a larger life. It is an intense feeling of life itself, and, in response to it, Oriard realized, "I felt expansive." This is the dilated self. For most people this level of being sinks below the horizon of consciousness and becomes a buried self that they know only in dreams, in love, and in sports. The athlete understands what Keats, perhaps the most concrete and sensuous of poets, meant when in one of his letters he exclaimed, "O for a Life of Sensations rather than of Thoughts!"[5]

As athletes discover that the body is a site of identity and as they listen to their bodies, what happens is a kind of learning from the inside out. Runner Lynda Huey's autobiography begins with an account of her performance in the 100-yard dash at the 1968 San Jose Women's Invitational Track and Field Meet, and she says that she knew she was going to run a good race because her body was telling

---

4. Michael Oriard, *The End of Autumn: Reflections on My Life in Football*, 196.
5. Ibid., 197. Keats, *Complete Poems and Selected Letters of John Keats*, 489. This idea is from Keats's November 22, 1817, letter to Benjamin Bailey.

her so. "Today, my legs are talking to me," she writes, "and saying only good things." In that meet she broke her personal record for best time, and her explanation was that her "body and mind have just totally expressed themselves." She knows from her personal experience, from those periods in her life when she was not exercising, that people who neglect the body turn it into a liability rather than what it is meant to be—"an instrument of expression."[6]

Lawrence Taylor, the Hall of Fame linebacker for the New York Giants, also learned from the inside out. He says he was never successful when he tried to "do things by the numbers." Instead, he "need[ed] to be free to follow this energy or this feeling or whatever you want to call it. . . . Technique has helped me along the way, but this invisible other thing has gotten me all the way from Lightfoot [his hometown in Virginia] to maybe one day hanging number 56 in the Hall of Fame." This inner spirit that he followed is something more than instinct; it is the daimonic, which he calls "wildness": "I seem to get this energy by following the wildness that's inside me rather than the rule book or playbook."[7] Taylor's "wildness" is the untamed part of the self, a vital dynamism that acts as a gemlike flame within the body.

To learn from the inside out is to experience an intensity characteristic of participation in sports. This intensity gives athletes a sense of what Lawrence Taylor uses as the subtitle of his autobiography: "Living on the Edge." Similar accounts by a wide variety of athletes all point to the same conclusion or interpretation: If "the echoing green" the athlete inhabits constitutes a Romantic construction of life, then the "dynamic organicism" that literary scholar Morse Peckham identifies as the main trait of Romanticism is, in the case of the athlete, located in the body itself.[8] To trace the athlete's "myth of origins" to its source also means to turn to the body or, more precisely, to his or her subjective experience of the body and the way he or she reads the text of the body.

Athletes are performers who speak with the body. As we have seen in the previous chapter, sports is a cult in part because its privileged initiates share a "language" with its own magical spell. The power of

6. Huey, *A Running Start*, 4, 7, 138.
7. Taylor and Falkner, *L.T.*, 190, 191.
8. Morse Peckham, *The Triumph of Romanticism*, 11, 34.

this special language—this "body song"—is so great that, in concert with youth, it often makes the athlete feel invincible. Although we traditionally conceptualize immortality as an indefinite extension of the time line stretching forward until it passes beyond the horizon and recedes toward infinity, we may also conceive of immortality as life rising above itself—a heightened sense of existence. In this conception, to be a god is not to live forever, but to live as we imagine the gods do. The subjective feelings of intensity, "wildness," and expansiveness that Taylor, Oriard, and others describe attest to this concept of immortality. In *Nothing But Net* Bill Walton attaches his love of basketball to the feeling that "you think you can do anything." What made the UCLA basketball teams that Kareem Abdul-Jabbar played on so great was not just their talent but their feeling that they inhabited what he calls in *Giant Steps* a special "cocoon of invincibility." Mike Ditka, the Chicago Bears tight end known as "Iron Mike," justifies the fans' nickname when he writes in his autobiography, "I thought I was indestructible." The body's daimonic energy has the power to create the feelings these athletes write about. As Mickey Mantle described himself after his first World Series with the Yankees, "I was twenty years old and I thought I was superman."[9] This indomitableness of spirit is the gift of the great athlete graced with an extraordinary body.

• "A Brotherhood of Mutilation": The Body as Index of Mortality

We cannot miss, however, that both Ditka's and Mantle's statements resound with their sense of mortality. When athletes read their bodies, the text intimates immortality but also the shadow that belies it. Athletes glory in the power and grace of their extraordinary bodies, but their intimacy with their bodies registers with at least equal strength when they injure them. No matter how great the athlete, their autobiographies reveal that their playing days are filled with pressure and fear. There is the pressure always to perform at the

9. For this conception of immortality, see Michael Novak, "American Sports, American Virtues," 37. Walton and Wojciechowski, *Nothing but Net*, 249. Abdul-Jabbar and Knobler, *Giant Steps*, 162. Mike Ditka and Don Pierson, *Ditka: An Autobiography*, 123. Mickey Mantle and Herb Gluck, *The Mick*, 79.

highest level of excellence, to continue to have a legitimate claim to the identity they have created with their bodies, whether it be as "Iron Mike," Hakeem "The Dream" Olajuwon, or Nolan Ryan, "The Ryan Express." And there is the constant fear that at any moment an injury will immediately end their careers forever. The huge size and great speed of today's outstanding athletes have made sports exciting but also more dangerous for the participants. As Charles Barkley points out, "My body was not meant to play the way I do. . . . if I couldn't play with pain, I wouldn't be playing at all." While accounts of injuries are a staple of most autobiographies, they dominate or become one of the main subjects of many autobiographies. Former Dallas Cowboys football player Pete Gent was right when he wrote in his novel *North Dallas Forty* that the players compose a "brotherhood of mutilation."[10]

The brotherhood's code—another sign of the cult—rests upon their belief in the necessity of playing with pain. But their pride in "playing hurt" masks a deeper-seated fear. In *The End of Autumn* Michael Oriard's analysis of his Kansas City Chiefs teammates is that their motivation for playing with pain is based not only on courage but on the need to transcend the limitations of human frailty. He argues that professional football players are terrified by their own mortality and that an incapacitating injury forebodes the end of their careers. Other athletes remark in their autobiographies that injured players are ignored and sometimes treated almost if they were lepers by the coaches and even their own teammates. This behavior springs from their fears and their self-protective avoidance of these reminders of what lies in wait for them, too. In *Ball Four* Jim Bouton talks about the close association of pain and fear and remarks that players usually do not tell their teammates about their injuries because it might get back to the coaches. "More important," he adds, "it's because you don't want to admit it to yourself."[11]

If some sports autobiographies are cast in the form of heroic epics, then the traditional convention called the epic catalogue is found in their long lists of serious injuries. One of the most graphic and revealing catalogues is found in the autobiography of Bob Chandler, a

10. Barkley and Johnson, *Outrageous!* 267, 269. Peter Gent, *North Dallas Forty,* 161.
11. Bouton and Shecter, *Ball Four,* 48.

former wide receiver for the Oakland Raiders. The first sentence of *Violent Sundays* is "Please, God, I don't want to die!"[12] Chandler was in the intensive care unit at a Denver hospital just after the opening game of the 1981 season. A Denver Broncos player hit Chandler so hard that the impact from the blow mangled his metal face mask. A sonogram revealed more than a gallon of blood floating in his abdomen. After the doctors removed his spleen, they told him that the only reason the injury did not kill him was that he was in such good condition. Despite this near-death experience he continued to play football, and before he retired he tore a ligament, fractured a foot, and had surgery on his "good" knee. This was his ninth surgery due to football injuries. Because of all the injuries, Chandler's pregame ritual included a shot of Xylocaine, Indocin, and "bennies" (amphetamines).

Why would someone abuse his body in this way? Chandler was no "dumb jock." He was an intelligent person who wrote poetry, had his own radio show, acted, and earned a law degree. Chandler's answer to the question of why he played with so many injuries draws together many aspects of the complex interplay between the athlete's body and his identity. Despite several knee surgeries, "[w]hen you're young and strong," he writes, "you feel indestructible." But the attraction football had for him went beyond the pleasure he found in its physicality. It became associated for him with matters of gender and self-image. Off the field he was quiet, laid back, reserved, and very shy, but football gave him a tough-guy identity and convinced people he was special. He believed that "[b]ecause of the punishment I had endured and the comebacks I had mounted, there was no question concerning my masculinity." He kept coming back from all the injuries, enduring the grueling rehabilitations, taking the shots and other drugs because "football and being a player had become my personality."[13]

A version of this story appears in many sports autobiographies, and football players like Bob Chandler do not have an exclusive copyright to it. Despite winning several championships in both college and the NBA, Bill Walton saw his career as "a great wasteland of failure" because of all his basketball injuries. He endured thirty surgeries, and his autobiography begins at the end, with him crawling

12. Chandler and Fox, *Violent Sundays*, 9.
13. Ibid., 66, 150.

across his patio when he reinjured his knee and was unable to walk after attempting yet another comeback. The third chapter of Joe DiMaggio's *Lucky to Be a Yankee* establishes as one of its recurring themes his physical bad luck, the injuries that transformed the "wonder" into the "cripple." And after his loss to Irish Bob Murphy, boxer Jake La Motta confessed, "I had lost that self-image of indestructibility. I guess I was beginning to turn into an ordinary human, and to see myself this way frightened me." La Motta was not just listening to his body; he was reading it and he did not like what he learned. Michael Oriard had a similar experience when he injured his knee in high school. He saw his lame leg as a "grotesque *thing* grafted on to my body—like victims of elephantiasis I had seen pictured in *Time* magazine."[14] The intimacy between these athletes and their bodies has been lost, and along with it comes the loss of a crucial aspect of their identities—literally the "embodiment" of their identities. This, too, is learning from the inside out. For the athlete, the body is the self and biology is destiny, but, paradoxically, like Oriard's lame leg, it may, without warning, become an alien "other" than self.

• Well-Toned and Well-Tuned: The Body as Other

Like other entertainers and celebrities, athletes must negotiate a double consciousness. As performers, they are both subject and object, and if, in one sense, an athlete's body is his or her self, from another perspective it is an object, both to the fans and sometimes even to the athlete as well. Athletes sometimes experience their bodies as an "instrument" of the self. The Greek ideal of sports was that it was a form of self-creation and self-expression. If we extrapolate from this view, then the athlete is a kind of artist who takes a vision in his mind— think of how commonly athletes speak of visualizing what they are about to do—and performs it with his body.[15] Conceived of in this way, sports was probably the first performance art. In the following

14. Walton and Wojciechowski, *Nothing but Net*, 10. Joe DiMaggio, *Lucky to Be a Yankee*, 45. Jake La Motta, Joseph Carter, and Peter Savage, *Raging Bull: The True Story of a Champ*, 210. Oriard, *The End of Autumn*, 45.
   15. Giamatti, *Take Time for Paradise*, 40.

chapter I will develop this idea when I comment on the "physical genius" of athletes.

Bill Russell, the all-pro center on the Boston Celtics dynasty of the
1950s and 1960s, offers a good example of the ability of "physical genius" to translate mental images into bodily performance when in
his memoir *Second Wind* he explains his development into a great
player. He had very little athletic talent as a youngster. He confesses
that he couldn't even make his homeroom basketball team in ele-
mentary school, initially failed to make the high school team, and
later suffered the embarrassment of being the sixteenth player on a
fifteen-member team who had to share a uniform with a teammate.
He was, however, a fine student and he learned the technique of visualization by studying paintings. After his senior year in high school
he played on a touring team, and he began to transfer his ability to
visualize to basketball. On the team's long bus rides he would replay
the previous games with what he calls his "mental camera" and visualize himself doing what he had watched other players do. Joan
Benoit, the winner of the first women's marathon in the Olympics,
spent years training her body to perform superhuman feats, and the
self-image she chooses in her autobiography *Running Tide* is that she
"was like an artist who crafts a masterpiece over the course of ten
years." Metaphors that imply this view of the body are common in
sports autobiographies. For example, in *Reggie* former Oakland A's
and New York Yankees star Reggie Jackson refers to his eyes,
strength, and coordination as his "instruments," and in *Spencer Haywood: The Rise, the Fall, the Recovery* the former Olympic and professional basketball star compares his body to a violin.[16]

Frequently, the metaphor of choice reflects the technical expertise
and professionalization of modern sports rather than the older aesthetic ideal. Joan Benoit may view the body as a product of the athlete's creativity, but she also conceives of it as a machine: "It's as if I'm
an inventor; I created this body and now I'm watching it work. Any
glitches in the moving parts? (No.) Are the pumps and valves leak-
ing? (No.) Is there too much stress anywhere? (Not yet.)." Baseball

16. Bill Russell and Taylor Branch, *Second Wind: The Memoirs of an Opinionated
Man*, 72. Benoit and Baker, *Running Tide*, 174. Jackson and Lupica, *Reggie*, 93.
Spencer Haywood and Scott Osler, *Spencer Haywood: The Rise, the Fall, the Recov-
ery*, 163.

pitcher Jim Brosnan uses the same image in his diary: "My arm worked like a well-oiled machine. The batter came to the plate. My experience classified him. My mind told my arm what to do. And it did it." In *Rebound*, his first autobiography written two years before the better-known *Bad as I Wanna Be*, Dennis Rodman employs a video-game image to describe his performance on the court: "sometimes it feels like my body is out on the court but my mind is up in the stands controlling my body with a joystick."[17]

The image of the machine also comments on athletes' views of the relationship between the mind and the body. There are two basic conceptions of this relationship but little consensus among athletes about which is the more accurate. For some athletes, the body is a mere automaton carrying out their will. Gymnast Mary Lou Retton expresses this view the most directly: "You have to prepare your mind early so you know what's coming and your body just does it." Chris Evert, who was renowned for her mechanical baseline tennis game, attributes her style to "training the body to obey the mind." And champion diver Greg Louganis's practice routine was based upon what dancers call kinetic memory. "I memorized each routine so well," he writes in *Breaking the Surface*, "that my body could do it without my even thinking about it." On the other hand, in *Lady Bullfighter* Patricia McCormick conceives of the body as taking on a life of its own when she describes practicing until the body functions independently of thought. Marathon swimmer Diana Nyad offers a similar view in her autobiography *Other Shores*. She describes the techniques that foster pure mental focus, which, paradoxically, allows the body to "act freely and intuitively as you have devotedly taught it, without interference from the conscious mind."[18] Her language suggests that the body is almost like a child lovingly instructed by her mother until she is ready to perform on her own. Other athletes imply that the body as a creative emanation of the self is like a child when they talk about "pampering" their bodies.

17. Benoit and Baker, *Running Tide*, 104–5. Jim Brosnan, *The Long Season*, 186. Dennis Rodman, Pat Rich, and Alan Steinberg, *Rebound: The Dennis Rodman Story*, 224.

18. Mary Lou Retton, Bela Karolyi, and John Powers, *Mary Lou: Creating an Olympic Champion*, 11. Chris Evert Lloyd and Neil Amdur, *Chrissie: My Own Story*, 74. Greg Louganis and Eric Marcus, *Breaking the Surface*, 18. Nyad, *Other Shores*, 111–12.

Although the athletes present these metaphors as positive conceptualizations of the relationship between self and body, they are also
acts of reading the body that imply a dissociation that may become
very problematic and troubling. They reveal that the athlete's identity is tied up with his body, his physical existence, but at the same
time he is detached from his body. His consciousness is in part located in his body, but he is also conscious of his body as an object.

As we shall see in a later chapter, this dissociation often creates a
painful dilemma for the aging athlete, but it can also be a problem for
athletes in their prime, particularly in certain sports. In extreme
sports the athlete's success often depends specifically upon dissoci-
ating the body from the mind. In *Other Shores,* marathon swimmer
Diana Nyad, who swam in the freezing Great Lakes as well as warm-
water distances of sixty grueling miles, admits, "My head was willing to permit my body any and every abuse." Similarly, when the
pain of running a marathon got severe for Joan Benoit, she threw on
what she calls a high concentration "switch": "I forget I have a body;
I don't feel pain."[19]

The often brutal contact of football sometimes causes those players to experience a strange relationship between the self and the
body. Dave Meggysey was known as "Super Psyche" because of his
violent hits, but his use of his body as a weapon made him realize
"paradoxically, how cut off and removed I was from my body. . . . I
had used it and thought of it as a machine, a thing that had to be well-
oiled, well-fed, and well-taken-care of, to do a specific job."[20] The conversion experience he describes in *Out of Their League* is psychological
as well as political, and he says one of the reasons he gave up football
was because he finally lost the "will" to hit. Someone we would assume was less likely to feel this way about the body is Jerry Kramer,
one of the stars of the great Green Bay Packer championship teams of
the 1960s. He is a crew-cut straight arrow whose diary *Instant Replay*
is continually shadowed by the presence of his father figure, Coach
Vince Lombardi. Even his need for Lombardi's approval was not
strong enough to make him like body contact. In an interesting passage about his distaste for hitting, he transfers his feelings about contact to his helmet:

19. Nyad, *Other Shores,* 127. Benoit and Baker, *Running Tide,* 55.
20. Meggysey, *Out of Their League,* 197.

I hate my helmet. I've always hated it, I guess. You'd imagine that a person would become accustomed to wearing a helmet after eighteen years of football, but I've never really learned to live with it. After every offensive play of every game I play, I immediately undo the chin strap to my helmet. . . . I'm not going to throw away my helmet, though, because it's a good weapon, probably the best weapon I've got."[21]

His ambivalent feelings about his helmet reflect the strained relationship between his body and self. He almost compulsively loosens its contact with his head as soon as possible, but he knows he needs it and values it despite his uneasiness with his intimate relationship with it.

Kramer's experience of his body approaches what Meggysey explicitly identifies as his "schizophrenic" life in football, a divided sensibility that he captures vividly in *Out of Their League* when he describes running into his defensive line coach when he dropped by the stadium during the off-season:

> . . . he grabbed a hold of me and began shaking my hand. He pulled me close and I felt his left hand running over my body. I had two very strange feelings go through me while he was touching me and asking, "How's your weight, you workin' out, you gettin' in shape, you look a little thin." The first one was a repugnance at being handled like a piece of meat; the second was a warm feeling because he was expressing "fatherly" concern about me. It was a sort of psychological civil war.[22]

Meggysey's main issues in the autobiography are political—his success in football had always been a source of his self-image, but he had come to see America's glorification of the violence of football as an expression of the dehumanizing values that also led to our involvement in Vietnam—but the telling point is that he reads the issues in the expressive responses of his body. His body instinctively tells him who he is—a "son" who deeply needs the approval of his "father," the coach—but his political education in the anti-war movement has also taught him that his body is not his self but rather "a piece of meat," an object to be used and discarded by authorities, whether they be coaches or military officers.

21. Kramer and Shaap, *Instant Replay*, 80.
22. Meggysey, *Out of Their League*, 198.

The relationship between body and identity that these athletes describe reveals the tensions, ambiguities, and paradoxes found in their larger constructions of the world of sports. At their best, athletes speak with their bodies: the word is made flesh. They are all one energy. They claim the admiration of the fan in his armchair in part because they are not subject to the mind-body split that their marvelous performances remind him is too often his problem. Their testimony is that the mind's images work best when idea expresses itself in doing. On the other hand, their greater intimacy with their bodies leads them to read their bodies, and the very act creates a distance between self and body. The paradox is that the body is both a manifestation of identity and a medium or signifier of the self that bespeaks its separateness from the self.

- **The Body as Text:**
  The Special Cases of Gendered and Racialized Bodies

If the body is a text that the athlete reads as well as a text that he "performs"—a "body song"—he soon discovers that the interests of fans include their own ways of reading his body. The centrality of the body is such that the public has always read it in a variety of ways. Phrenologists read the conformation of the skull, and palm readers interpret the "life lines" on the hand. In the nineteenth century physiognomy, the practice of discovering qualities of character by studying the face and body, was considered a legitimate scientific method. We may distrust these folk strategies and pseudo-sciences as superstitious nonsense, but we are less likely to dismiss out of hand the idea that biology is destiny or to slight the doctor's "art" in conducting a physical "examination." The pervasiveness of the view that the body is a cultural text is evident, even if subconscious, in such everyday activities as "reading" someone's "body language." A part of our fascination with sports is that athletes are larger-than-life figures in the literal sense of these words. In their extraordinary bodies we find some of our cultural issues writ large.

One of the most obvious ways in which the body is a marker of cultural values is its reflection of the contemporary concern for fitness and health. We are struck when we watch classic black-and-white movies of the 1940s and 1950s by the omnipresence of the cigarette,

and by contrast those rare occasions in recent movies when the attractive lead actor smokes have made some viewers suspicious that
it represents an unscrupulous form of product placement by the to-
bacco industry. A memorable *New Yorker* cartoon from the 1970s pictured a huge, ant-like stream of runners crossing a bridge during the
running of the New York Marathon, and the caption ran, "What ever
happened to the loneliness of the long distance runner?" We live in
an era of personal trainers, health clubs, and baby carriages designed
to speed along as they are propelled ahead by jogging mothers. It is
an era in which a "six pack" sometimes refers to well-defined stom-
ach muscles. Perhaps, as some cynics claim, the only remaining sin is
to be fat. These are again signs of the body as an aspect of identity, but
they also suggest our view of the body as an object, an "other."

• The Gaze: The Male Athlete as Miss America

While the body may be an instrument for the athlete, it cannot escape the culture of consumption in which we live. Athletes, particularly when sports becomes entertainment for the public, become
objectified by the gaze of the fan in the way that women are often
viewed in this way by men, and for some of the same reasons. There
is an undeniable erotic element in sports, in watching the performances of young men and women with extraordinary bodies. Because
basketball players are more scantily dressed than their counterparts
in football and baseball and the size of the arenas in which they play
creates a more intimate atmosphere than is possible in stadiums, they
are acutely aware of being sex objects for their fans.

It is not surprising that in *Bad as I Wanna Be* Dennis Rodman would
revel in being the "Madonna of the NBA" and pose as the sensitive
person offended by being exploited as a commodity, "the best pros-
titute in a high-class whorehouse." In his basketball diary, *Life on the
Run*, Bill Bradley analyzes the way the New York Knicks fans read the
bodies of the players. It is significant, he points out, that the players
are "[u]nencumbered by masks, pads, or hats."[23] Although the players are celebrities and therefore familiar to the fans, Bradley thinks
the fans mistake that familiarity for knowledge of who the athletes

23. Rodman and Keown, *Bad as I Wanna Be*, 81. Bradley, *Life on the Run*, 111.

really are and create images that say more about their own lives than the athletes'. (It is interesting to note that sports fans' feelings of familiarity and intimacy with their favorite athletes allow them to refer to them by their first names—Wilt, Billie Jean, for example—something that they are not likely to do with other celebrities such as Donald Trump or movie stars like Tom Cruise or Julia Roberts.)

Bradley explains the particular form of objectification that the athlete experiences:

> A strong and inseparable bond exists between the innocent, beautiful girl and the pampered athlete. Both are objects in the eyes of most people. Both are given credit only for their physical attributes, and receive inordinate prizes for them. They are told they are something special, Miss America and the All-American, without understanding what qualities beyond the superficialities of face and body hold importance in life. . . . An athlete knows the world of a beautiful girl. Maybe that is why DiMaggio and Monroe stuck in the American imagination as an example of a mythic match.[24]

This treatment, which is based upon the athlete's extraordinary body and the particular brand of masculinity it models, massages his ego, but the thoughtful athlete can recognize that, like the attention he gets from women at courtside, it reflects an absence of interest in him as a person. But despite their dislike of being treated like a consumable product, most successful athletes exploit that appeal by marketing themselves as commercial products. At the lower end of the food cycle, they hawk themselves in selling everything from suits to automobiles, and the superstar athletes like Michael Jordan and David Beckham become mini-corporations and make far more money from their endorsement deals than from their sports salaries.

- **"There I Was, Forearms and All, Right Next to Olivia Newton John":
The Female Athlete and Gender Conflict**

For women, whether they were athletes or not, the body was traditionally considered the primary text of their lives. As the old epithet the "fairer sex" implies, they have traditionally been defined by their

24. Bradley, *Life on the Run*, 202.

bodies. Issues of the body dominate women's sports to a far greater degree than men's sports, ranging from earlier eras' fears that participation in strenuous sports would damage women's reproductive organs, to exclusion of women from certain sports such as long-distance running events because their bodies were not thought to be suitable for successful performance in them, to current debates about the aesthetics of female body-building. Once social mores allowed women athletes to shed the clothing that modesty rather than utility dictated, the erotic qualities of their body texts were an important feature of their sports performance. It is not a coincidence that the first Miss America pageant in 1921 was followed within a year by the first official recognition of the woman athlete, the establishment of the category of "Women as Athletes" in the *Reader's Guide to Periodical Literature*.[25] In the 1920s the "Ziegfeld Girls" on Broadway and the sports "goddesses" in tennis and ice skating were similar expressions of the commercialization of women's bodies. Despite the protests over *Sports Illustrated*'s annual swimsuit issue, its justification rests on the persistent importance of the eroticism of the female body in sports.

A key stage in the development of women's sports was Billie Jean King's pioneering efforts on behalf of the professional women's tennis tour in the 1970s, and she was very aware of the necessity of using the body, sex appeal, beauty, and the erotic to market the sport. In her autobiography she discusses the Women's Tennis Association's strategy:

> ... tennis is a very sexy sport, and that is good. The players are young, with excellent bodies, clothed in relatively little. It offers the healthiest, most appealing presentation of sex I can imagine, and we in the sport must acknowledge that and use it to our advantage. . . . In the WTA, we try to encourage our players to be as attractive and as feminine as possible. . . . The point is that appearance counts for a lot in any sport, but is perhaps even more important to tennis, where the fans are so close to the players.[26]

Her use of "presentation" is instructive. The body not only performs and entertains. It is also a product for consumption, and presentation is a key ingredient for the discerning consumer. In *The Education of a Woman Golfer* Nancy Lopez stresses the same point

25. Stephanie L. Twin, "Women and Sport," 207.
26. Billie Jean King and Frank Deford, *Billie Jean*, 146–48.

about golf. In the autobiography she discusses how important appearance is in pleasing the tour's sponsors. Women's professional golf has become big business, and looking attractive, she points out, is a necessary part of big business. Her personal conservatism prevents her from doing anything more than briefly mentioning allegations of lesbianism on the tour or problems created by the menstrual cycle, but she does single out the weight problem that many women on the tour have. King, Lopez, and their fellow professionals are well aware that their sports depend upon the way the public reads their bodies. Their athletic bodies—all the hours they spent exercising, training, and performing their bodies—are literally the "product" of their success.

Although the body of the female athlete is an important source of her identity, as it is for the male athlete, society's reading of her body often creates a role conflict or identity crisis. At least during the formative years of the women's movement in sports, the question was could a female be both a woman and an athlete. Huey, King, Navratilova, Evert, Nyad, Shriver, and their peers who write autobiographies all assert that they can, but the culture's gaze usually made their self-images a difficult and painful construction. Pam Shriver, a thoughtful tennis player who at the time she wrote *Passing Shots* was being groomed by the Republican Party for a possible career in politics, blames the serious problems with bulimia that a number of women on the tour have on the sports lifestyle, which "places such a premium on our looks and health that we become more vulnerable to emotional problems."[27]

These players are caught between the need to build strong bodies if they are to be competitive in the sport and society's equation of beauty with thinness rather than strength. Marathoner Joan Benoit was a wonderful all-around athlete, but around the sixth grade, she remembers, her love of sports went "underground." The impact of the women's movement made it possible for girls to think about careers in medicine and law, but Benoit says that girls still believed "we shouldn't want muscles."[28] It is clear that, for all the benefits we enjoy

27. For a more detailed discussion of the issue of gender conflict in the lives of Billie Jean King and Lynda Huey, see James W. Pipkin, "Life on the Cusp: Lynda Huey and Billie Jean King." Shriver, Deford, and Adams, *Passing Shots*, 94.
28. Benoit and Baker, *Running Tide*, 43.

from the great social advances of the second half of the twentieth century, cultural taboos about the body have not disappeared.

Martina Navratilova's story typifies the dilemma faced by many women athletes. The culture's traditional reading of the female body equated it with softness and weakness rather than strength, inertia rather than movement, and passivity rather than aggression. In short, the culture identified sports with masculine qualities, depriving women of much of the legitimacy for participation in sports. Their bodies were constructed differently from men's, the common view went, and certainly they were "constructed" differently by the assumptions of the culture. We see the cultural construction emblemized in the Victorian ideal of woman. This "product" of the nineteenth century, which persisted in subliminal if not explicit ways well into the twentieth century, was epitomized by one of two models: the "Pre-Raphaelite Damozel" with her Eve-like lips, erotic swan's neck, and pale tubercular beauty (the painter Burne-Jones once described his models as "female heads with floral adjuncts"); and "The Angel in the House," an image that disembodied the woman in favor of an ethereal but sexless spirit.

Navratilova describes in her autobiography the chasm between her body and society's conception of the feminine. She remembers "at thirteen I had no hair on my body except on my head. I was very slow in reaching puberty, had no breasts, and didn't until I was fourteen or fifteen, and naturally I wondered if there was something wrong with me."[29] She also recounts the painful memory of going to the movies with her grandmother and, despite her protests, being sent by the ladies' room attendant to the men's room. This was not an isolated incident; people were always mistaking her for a boy. She had no figure—her father's nickname for her was "Prut," Czech for "stick"— and was self-conscious about her big calves, big ears, and big feet, all of which made her fear that she was always going to look like a boy.

This reading of her body was exacerbated when she left Czechoslovakia for America. Here she violated another taboo about the feminine body when she gained a lot of weight. She engaged in what she calls a "well-known . . . love affair with the fast food emporiums of

29. Martina Navratilova and George Vecsey, *Martina*, 87.

the New World," and when she put on twenty pounds during her first month in America sportswriters derided her as "The Great Wide Hope" and described her eating habits as if she were on a mission to consume as many Big Macs as she could. America's reading of her body created a dilemma for her. "I didn't know exactly who I wanted to look like," she explains, "but I definitely wanted to look more feminine. I couldn't do much about it, though, couldn't just chop down my muscles. They were in the genes."[30]

Her response to society's view of her body is interesting, but it did not resolve the issue underlying her conflicted feelings. On the one hand, she tried to conform. She lost weight, had her hair lightened to blonde, took makeup lessons at Vidal Sassoon's salon in New York, and used eye liner and blush to heighten her high Slavic cheekbones. As a result, she says, "I started liking the way I looked in the summer of 1981. I was a far cry from the little girl her father called Prut." On the other hand, she began a serious conditioning and weight-lifting routine that made her a powerful athlete. *Time* magazine used her in a cover story about the new concept of femininity and the ideal of being in shape rather than merely shapely, but her reaction to her picture is telling: "There I was, forearms and all, right next to Olivia Newton John." Her pride in her body could not totally block out her continuing uneasiness about the traditional image of femininity represented by the beautiful movie star in the photograph. Despite the cosmetic makeover, the public read her body and still saw primarily her powerful musculature. "I'm the Goliath," she admits in her autobiography. She clearly feels that the image connotes something far more disturbing than her powerful tennis game because later in the autobiography she laments that she is seen as "some oversized monster looming over the women's tour."[31] The metaphors capture the stigma that until recently most serious women athletes had to face. The implication goes beyond the view that if they are athletes they are too masculine to be women. What Navratilova and many other women athletes had to confront was that the culture viewed their bodies as unnatural and them as freaks.

The woman's traditional role was to inhabit the domestic sphere, and in sports the domestic sphere's equivalent was recreational

30. Ibid., 2, 54.
31. Ibid., 240, 59, 71, 287.

sports. The underlying philosophy of recreational sports was that they fostered health, fun, and social companionship for women. "Sports for sports' sake" represents the purest concept of play, but in the case of women's sports it was intended to exclude the idea of competition and the ideal of mastery over one's body.[32] Serious women athletes such as Lynda Huey were left unfulfilled by what she calls the "cookies and punch" mentality that dominated recreational sports for women. As early as the 1930s Babe Didrikson had ignored the cultural norms in her desire to play basketball and compete in the Olympics, and an entrepreneur's effort to stage a race between her and a horse is an example of the public's perception that mannish women like the Babe—"tomboy" was the stereotypical epithet— were strange creatures to be exhibited in events that smacked of the carnival sideshow. Despite her willingness to transgress the acceptable bounds for women on the playing field, however, when Babe—now married and publicly known as Babe Zaharias—published her 1955 autobiography *This Life I've Led*, she felt pressure to counter rumors about her mannishness and sexual orientation by constructing "an acceptable version of a female athlete's life. . . . It is not, at times, the life she led."[33]

Martina Navratilova also dramatically challenged society's views of women athletes, not just with her public admission of her bisexuality but also with the obvious results of her weight training. In her autobiography she proudly admits, "Sure, my forearms are bigger than the other women players', but I didn't get them in a five-and-dime store. . . . It's like the advertisement says: I got my muscles 'the old-fashioned way.' I earned them." At the same time she confesses that she resented all the jokes about her being "the first bionic tennis player," an allusion to a popular television series of the time about a woman who was so seriously injured skydiving that parts of her body had to be reconstructed with mechanical parts. This

32. For more information about views of women and sport, see Twin's essay cited above and Allen Guttmann's *Women's Sports: A History* and his chapter "Women's Sports" in *A Whole New Ball Game*, 139–58.

33. Susan E. Cayleff, *Babe: The Life and Legend of Babe Didrikson Zaharias*, 5. In an earlier article, "The 'Texas Tomboy': The Life and Legend of Babe Didrikson Zaharias," Cayleff mentions that in particular Zaharias included numerous examples of dating boys, marriage proposals, and comments about her domestic skills, many of them "grossly exaggerated or fictitious," 31.

reading of her body hurts her because she says it makes her "sound like something slightly different from the rest of humanity."[34] The issue here goes beyond that of the woman as "other." In reading her body and comparing her to Goliath and a bionic creature, society implies that she is less than the rest of humanity, or at least less than a woman, as well as different from the rest of humanity. The identity that society usually inscribes for women athletes with powerful bodies is that of the freak.

As Leslie Fiedler argues in his book about freaks, women are viewed as freaks when their bodies appear to transgress what the culture perceives as the natural boundaries between what is female and what is male.[35] Many of the women athletes who have written autobiographies—Lynda Huey, Chris Evert, Diana Nyad, Patricia McCormick, Billie Jean King, Althea Gibson, for example—explicitly discuss the stigma that they or their peers have had to face because they are seen as freaks. Women athletes often have bodies that are aberrations from the norm, which in turn raises questions about their femininity, their happiness with their gender, and their sexual orientation.

The issue, once again, goes back to the role conflict women athletes have historically faced, the question of whether they can be both an athlete and a woman. In her book on the culture of disability, Rosemarie Garland Thomson also points out that there is a historical justification for the conceptual link between women and freaks. According to Thomson, traditionally

> . . . the freak is represented much like the woman: both are owned, managed, silenced, and mediated by men; both are socially defined as deviations from the ideal masculine body; both are marginalized in the realm of economic production; both are appropriated for display as spectacles; both are seen as subjugated by the body.[36]

Billie Jean King says that female athletes of her generation grew up with the burden of lacking approval from much of society because they were often viewed as "mannish freaks."[37] For King, the problem

34. Navratilova and Vecsey, *Martina*, 273, 278.
35. Leslie Fiedler, *Freaks: Myths and Images of the Secret Self*, 24.
36. Rosemarie Garland Thomson, *Extraordinary Bodies: Figuring Physical Disability in American Culture and Literature*, 70–71.
37. King and Deford, *Billie Jean*, 89.

was compounded by the way she read her own body. What she saw, as if they leaped out from her other features like a three-dimensional movie, was her bad eyesight, her fat legs, and her breathing problems. Her fellow tennis pro Pam Shriver was self-conscious about her six-foot height, which she says intimidated men, and her "duck-footed" body. Althea Gibson, who in 1957 became the first black to win Wimbledon and the U.S. Nationals, writes in *I Always Wanted to Be Somebody* that she was ostracized as a freak by the girls because she did not know how to do the things girls did but played football and baseball with the boys. And Lynda Huey confesses that all her life she felt like a freak. She writes that female runners in the late 1960s were not considered to be legitimate athletes, and the public looked at them as if they were "specimens in a sideshow." The image objectifies women and, worse, stigmatizes them as monstrous prodigies in a carnival exhibit.[38]

Huey predicted in her 1976 autobiography that the next generation of women athletes would benefit from new ideals of femininity that were the product of society's increasing emphasis on health and fitness, and recent surveys have indicated that contemporary women athletes no longer experience this role conflict or feel stigmatized. While the motto of the early Virginia Slims Women's Tennis Tour—"You've come a long way, Baby!"—is undoubtedly true, we should caution ourselves about too easily dismissing the old attitudes as relics of an unenlightened past. As some arguments about the role violence plays in the popularity of pro football suggest, people's feelings about their bodies are often too deeply seated to yield completely to the claims of sweet reason. Even articles celebrating the new healthy and fit muscular woman have not erased the culture's continuing preference for more traditional conceptions of female beauty.

Another athlete of the 1980s, Olympic gymnast Mary Lou Retton, reveals some of the same ambivalent feelings about her body. In her autobiography she presents herself as the new breed of woman athlete who has revolutionized her sport, but her reading of her own body betrays some conflicting emotions. She is obviously proud of her strength, referring to her "Body by U.S. Steel." On the other hand,

38. Huey, *A Running Start,* 125.

she cannot be completely satisfied if she sees her build as "constructed like a cast-iron toy truck." The imagery is reminiscent of the bionic android that Navratilova had to endure as her identity, and the diminutive toy serves to trivialize her as well as point to her short stature. A few pages later she contextualizes this body portrait with a childhood memory that seems more honest than her initial avowals. Like many other young girls, she took ballet lessons but her build kept her from being a graceful dancer. This realization was so painful that she cried when she was forced to admit it. "I can't be what they want me to be," she remembers thinking. "But there was nothing I could do about it," she adds. "I just didn't fit the classical mold. I was short and muscular and a good all-round athlete."[39]

Tracy Austin, a tennis star whose career extended into the 1990s, was a Chris Evert clone in looks as well as playing style—short, cute, feminine, the girl next door. Yet even she felt she had to hide the fact that she lifted weights. Her opinion about cultural views of the female athlete's body, which she expressed in her 1992 autobiography *Beyond Center Court,* is that "I hope there will be a time when it will be acceptable for women to play sports without ever being thought of as masculine, but I don't think we're entirely there yet."[40] Even the glorious triumph of the U.S. women's soccer team in the 1999 World Cup was filled with messages and images that indirectly reinforced traditional views of femininity. There were reminders of the "goddesses" of the 1920s as Brandi Chastain posed almost completely nude in a magazine and struck an erotic if powerful pose as she stripped off her jersey top after scoring the winning goal in the championship game shoot-out. The television broadcasters singled out the players' feminine beauty and their heterosexual interests such as their relish for the conjugal visits they were allowed in training camp, and a prominent television commercial focused on the entire team going on a date with a lucky young man. There were also frequent observations about the two married women on the team and sideline shots of their children and husbands. And of course Mia Hamm became everyone's pin-up girl, praised almost as much for her traditional beauty as for her explosive skills on the field. Clearly,

39. Retton, Karolyi, and Powers, *Mary Lou,* xiii, xiv, 12.
40. Austin and Brennan, *Beyond Center Court,* 204.

these women were not Amazons, and the television commercial featuring a series of competitions between Mia Hamm and Michael Jordan contained an erotic appeal that left no room for suspicions about any mannishness of her body.

It may be true that women are no longer intruders in the world of sports, but such is the belatedness of their arrival there that their confidence about the female body's complete freedom from the old stereotypical constructions may suggest the lady doth sometimes protest too much.

- ## "Nobody Roots for Goliath": The Black Giant as Domesticated Freak

We also find particularly dramatic examples of the cultural construction of the body when we turn from matters of gender to matters of race. For blacks, sports may have offered more democratic opportunities than other institutions did, but its history of racial quotas and stacking—the practice in football of grouping blacks in those positions believed to depend upon strength and speed rather than intelligence—reveals that it established its own versions of Jim Crow. The plantation ethos continued to manifest itself, in the view of many blacks, in matters centering on the body. Jackie Robinson strikes the general theme when he writes in *I Never Had It Made* that black ballplayers were valued for their "bodies, the physical stamina, the easy reflexes" but were believed to be "lacking in the gray matter that it supposedly takes to serve as managers, officials, and executives in policy-making positions."[41]

In *Long Time Coming* former NBA star Chet Walker compares college recruitment to a "slave auction, where bodies and health were everything."[42] Even more visceral are the sensations described by athletes such as Walker, Muhammad Ali in *The Greatest*, and Satchel Paige in *Pitchin' Man* when, as they relate, their treatment made them feel like racehorses. Although many fans marveled at the exploits of "the ageless Satchel Paige," as he was called, he mentions in his autobiography that he was examined on several occasions as if he were

41. Robinson and Duckett, *I Never Had It Made*, 258–59.
42. Chet Walker and Chris Messenger, *Long Time Coming: A Black Athlete's Coming-of-Age in America*, 51.

a horse to determine his age. Walker and Ali use the same comparison to register their feelings about the way their bodies were read: as powerful, perhaps even beautiful, animals rather than as fully human beings.

Like other performers and entertainers, these athletes were commodities, the property of the team owners. But, compared to the resentment of white athletes, the pain with which black athletes recount their experiences is compounded by the legacy of slavery that contextualizes their experiences. The corrosive legacy of the plantation tradition imbues their feelings with an additional dimension. As Chet Walker confesses in *Long Time Coming*—a title that places his personal story against the canvas of the larger epic of racial consciousness—it creates an "uneasiness about ownership of their bodies."[43] For all its power and grace, the body of the black athlete can at times be a reminder of his "otherness." If injuries can alienate players like Jerry Kramer and Dave Meggysey from their own bodies, psychic scars from a racist past and present sometimes create a similar feeling for the black athlete.

Like women athletes, objectified black athletes often feel that the public views them as freaks. Since the determining factor is usually that of scale, basketball players are the athletes most commonly stigmatized in this way. Occasionally, the issue is size in the sense of weight. For example, in his autobiography *Outrageous!* Charles Barkley discusses the way he was "taunted as an over-weight freak" and ridiculed as the "Round Mound of Rebound" and "Boy Gorge."[44] The basis of the image is usually height, however. Current NBA players inhabit a land of giants. Not only was the starting lineup of the great Kentucky teams of the 1950s all-white, but they could also afford to have at least one forward who was only a little over six feet tall. Today even the guards are often six feet five to six feet nine, and seven-footers are commonplace on the front line. Probably the first basketball player to be stigmatized as a freak was George Mikan. At six feet ten inches, Mikan was the first of the great centers in the NBA. In his autobiography *Unstoppable,* he discusses having to endure being called a "monster," a "goon," and "Frankenstein," not only by the fans but by opposing coaches as well. When he played in the

43. Ibid.
44. Barkley and Johnson, *Outrageous!* 105, 104.

1940s and 1950s, he was a giant among men, even on the basketball court. He relates that he avoided college dances and other social events because of the stigma involved. He explains that most people of this era assumed that tall men were "gangly, awkward rubes, maybe not too bright."[45]

Although Mikan was white, it is significant that the image is most often used for black athletes—Wilt Chamberlain, Bill Russell, and Kareem Abdul-Jabbar, for example. This association also has historical precedence. As far back as the middle ages, people have used the concept of the freak to describe foreign races and the exotic person. In the nineteenth century, circus people commonly referred to the freak show as the "Nig show" because so many of the freaks were people of color. Rosemarie Garland Thomson concludes that "Freaks always appeared not just as monsters, but as gendered and racialized monsters."[46] If the bodies of female freaks such as the "Bearded Lady" transgressed the normal boundaries between male and female, the bodies of freaks like "The Wild Boy of Borneo" and "Joey the Dog-Faced Boy" transgressed the normal boundaries between the human and the animal. The circus presented extraordinary black bodies to the public and justified their prurient interest by asking them to determine whether these freaks were examples of the "missing link," that is, whether they were human or animal. The freaks in the sideshow were exhibited in the formal sense of that term. They were staged in a way that focused on them solely as bodies without the context of humanity and that treated them as a source of profit. The carnival freak show was basically another version of the slave auction that reduced blacks to an ambiguous status somewhere between that of a farm horse and a childlike man. This tradition of reading the body, particularly the black body, provides an important context for considering the image of the freak that we find in the autobiographies of the three greatest centers in the history of basketball: Bill Russell, Wilt Chamberlain, and Kareem Abdul-Jabbar.

In his memoir *Second Wind,* Russell's account of this image is brief but telling. He says he understands that he may think of himself as

45. George Mikan and Joseph Oberle, *Unstoppable: The Story of George Mikan, the First NBA Superstar,* 64, 15.

46. Thomson, *Extraordinary Bodies,* 63, 29. Thomson provides interesting historical information about the freak show, 56–63.

an "aloof king" but that others see him as "King Kong," a giant, black animal. He realizes that King Kong's problem "was not how he interpreted the white world but how the white world saw *him*"—how it read his body. He is a freak to the white audience that watches him perform on the court, but, even if he refuses to accept that particular image, he sees himself as a "misfit." He explains: "It's impossible to have a sense of yourself without reference to other people, and if you're different there's no convenient place to start. It's hard for me to understand other people because I see a distorted world." Later in the autobiography he suggests that this view of his body may also provide an entry into his psyche: "All of us have a place inside ourselves that we believe is ugly and grotesque, and this hidden place is the part of our personality hardest to acknowledge to others. . . . But that hidden place is the most human part of you." Here Russell turns the tables on the voyeurs at the freak show, arguing that what they see as his grotesqueness is a sign not of his subhumanness, but of his humanity. The rest of the autobiography can be read as a gradual process by which he tries to say of this extraordinary part of himself what Shakespeare's Prospero says to the monster Caliban: "this thing of darkness I / Acknowledge mine."[47]

Wilt Chamberlain devotes one of the early chapters of his autobiography to what he calls "the freak factor." He, too, tries to define himself against the backdrop of a world that would deny his humanity because of his extraordinary body. He argues that in sports, "blacks are looked on as superhuman (or subhuman?) athletes (animals?)." The situation is even worse for the black athlete who is also a giant. The public views him as a "brainless goon or sideshow freak." He is treated like "a monster from the deep, out to destroy their game, rape their wives, and eat their children alive." Chamberlain's imagery captures many of the traditional associations of the monster: violence, castration, cannibalism, revenge, and fear of counterrevenge. As Leslie Fiedler theorizes in his book about freaks, this concept also expresses our "primordial fears . . . about scale, sexuality, our status as more than beasts, and our tenuous individuality." Fiedler argues that because we were once small but will never be tall,

47. Russell and Branch, *Second Wind*, 189, 190, 235–36. Shakespeare, *The Tempest*, 130. This line appears in act V, scene 1, lines 275–76.

Giants are "inimicable others" with whom we cannot identify. As Chamberlain puts it, "Nobody roots for Goliath."[48]

The freak is sometimes represented as subhuman, at other times as nonhuman. Chamberlain quotes a newspaper column by Jim Murray of the *Los Angeles Times* that casts him in the image of the latter, a nonhuman creation of a mad Frankenstein: "He was put together in a laboratory by a mad doctor with a pair of pliers, a screwdriver and a Bunsen burner. If you look close, you can see the bolts in the forehead. You don't feed it, you oil it, baby." In Murray's column, we can almost hear the voice of the carnival barker asking the audience to read the body of the freak and reciting the words from the printed pamphlet that circus entrepreneurs like P. T. Barnum used to give a pseudo-historical account of the freak's origins. As Fiedler explains, the freak was sometimes the object of terror, but it was also an example of what Aristotle termed the *lusus naturae,* a joke of nature that suggested the ludicrous as well as the anomalous. In his autobiography Chamberlain confesses that what he fears most is the loss of dignity. He says that he hates his nickname "Wilt the Stilt" because "it makes me sound like an attraction in a carnival sideshow." He also relates that he decided not to go through with plans for a boxing match between him and Muhammad Ali because his accountant convinced him that he might "be embarrassed and humiliated and laughed at like some freak in a carnival sideshow."[49]

Chamberlain had to confront this image in the process of defining his own identity. The difficulty is that he understood that his extraordinary body was an essential aspect of his identity. One part of his solution was to name himself. In *Wilt* he writes that when he reads his body, he sees not "Wilt the Stilt" but "the Big Dipper," and he even inscribed the name *Ursa Major* on his house and his boat. It offers a different reading of his body. As he puts it, "it tells a story." It has "a certain beauty and power and grace and majesty—and it represents something real, enduring, eternal. . . . It's bigger than life itself." He argues that time and circumstance brought him his humanity, even in the eyes of the fans who had always booed him. He says he found in the last stage of his career that he had been "hu-

48. Chamberlain and Shaw, *Wilt,* 27, 215, 26, 77. Fiedler, *Freaks,* 96, 34, 92. Chamberlain and Shaw, *Wilt,* 34.

49. Chamberlain and Shaw, *Wilt,* 26. Fiedler, *Freaks,* 231. Chamberlain and Shaw, 28, 246.

manized" as the fans discovered his mortality in the form of a severe injury to his knee that slowed him but failed to incapacitate him, and in the even larger form of a new, young giant, Kareem Abdul-Jabbar.[50] While he could never become the little, human-scale David, Chamberlain believed he became an object for identification as the aging warrior combated on the basketball court the new symbol of "Mr. Evil," Abdul-Jabbar.

The title of Abdul-Jabbar's autobiography, *Giant Steps*, announces his recognition of his place in the carnival but also suggests his view that he successfully transformed the way in which the public should read his extraordinary body. Far from being an invulnerable physical power as a boy, Abdul-Jabbar was more like the classic "90-pound weakling." He confesses in *Giant Steps* that he lacked the instinct to fight and "used to get my ass handed to me on a daily basis." "I didn't have that many fights," he adds. "I just lost all of them." As he grew into a young giant, he was even less comfortable with his body. He says he felt "as if I were wearing somebody else's suit and kept tripping over the cuffs." It is no coincidence that his blackness and his freakishness or monstrosity were intertwined. His recognition that he was a giant came when he left New York City for a Philadelphia boarding school where he also discovered for the first time that he was darker than the other students: "I never felt like I was black until I was made to." His response to what at that time he perceived as a double stigma was to become the invisible man: "As big as I was, I simply tried not to be there."[51]

A brief but telling comment in his autobiography reveals that one way Abdul-Jabbar dealt with his dilemma was by imagining a transformation or conversion, using as his model his reading of the story of the ugly duckling that becomes a majestic black swan. For Abdul-Jabbar, this conversion began on the basketball court, but the actual site of the conversion was his body. Despite his awkwardness on the court, he learned that he was "totally at ease and inexplicably confident" when he shot his hook shot.[52] The "Giant Steps" of his title can be interpreted as the sense of identity that had its origins in his reading of his body and was later revealed in other forms such as his

50. Chamberlain and Shaw, *Wilt*, 28, 239.
51. Abdul-Jabbar and Knobler, *Giant Steps*, 1, 3, 18, 15, 17.
52. Ibid., 19.

discovery of black consciousness and his conversion to Islam. But the body provided the main text that unlocked the meaning of who he is: a majestic giant swan, not a grotesque animal.

The examples provided by the accounts of Russell, Chamberlain, and Abdul-Jabbar have two other implications about modern sports. First, the image of the freak points to the transformation of sports by business. The ritual sports hero—the pure athlete—still exists, but his heroic qualities are usually obscured by the spectacle that transforms sports into entertainment. It is appropriate that baseball players speak of reaching the big leagues as making it to "the show." At "the show," most athletes become celebrities rather than heroes. They make enormous salaries, but, in turn, they, like freaks, display their extraordinary bodies as a source of entertainment and profit. Like freaks, they are always presented or shown by a mediator, but in our era the mediator is not the priest, parent, scientist, doctor, or P. T. Barnum, but television. Black and women athletes, in particular, become modern-day versions of what Rosemarie Thomson calls "colonized" or "domesticated" freaks.[53] The body is not only their destiny but also the source of their self-image. It also creates a self-image that they sometimes must struggle to overcome.

That task becomes a central concern in some sports autobiographies written by blacks and women. The implications are more significant and personal when these athletes engage in the remembrance and reflection necessary for writing an autobiography. In writing about the process of self-making, they must confront the relation between visible bodily particularity and identity. Their initial reading of their extraordinary bodies often leaves them feeling stigmatized, silenced, and managed. Thomson explains that the freak embodies a "pure text" in the sense that it is "written in boldface to be deciphered according to the needs and desires of the onlookers." The great virtue of the act of writing an autobiography, however, is that it affords a second reading of experience, and, in this case, of the body. This process allows the thoughtful athlete to achieve what Jane Gallop, in exploring women's autobiographies, has called "thinking through the body." She argues that the split between the mind and the body "makes the mother into an inhuman monster by dividing the human

53. Thomson, *Extraordinary Bodies*, 66, 17.

realm of culture, history, and politics from the realm of love and the body where the mother carries, bears, and tends her children."[54] The thoughtful athlete's impulse is to overcome this split between the mind and the body because he, like the child-bearing mother, understands that the body is a site of knowledge, a medium for thought.

In the case of certain black basketball giants, the issue is their ability to read their extraordinary bodies not as the stigma a freak must bear but as a mark of overpowering distinction. They read their bodies as myths of ugly ducklings transformed into majestic black swans or as symbols of a sublime Ursa Major. For the women athletes, the resolution is not as reassuring. They do not sing a Whitmanesque song of "the body electric," but they do defiantly insist that their size or their muscles do not transgress the boundaries that separate female from male. They have adopted the feminist philosophy that women have distinctive identities, but, unlike feminists, they are not comfortable suggesting that in reading the female athlete's body we must be open to new concepts of beauty. They proudly read their bodies' strength and power, but the aesthetic issue often remains either a strained assertion or an uneasy question.

What links the autobiographies of both the males and the females, however, is that their bodies become "monstrous" in the original Latin sense of the word. The word "monster" is derived from *monstra*, which means "sign," and it forms the root of *demonstrare*, "to show." In writing about their lives, athletes realize that their extraordinary bodies are "monstrous births," not in the sense that they are grotesque freaks but in the sense that they "show forth" their destinies and serve as oracles that can be read or interpreted as holding the secrets of the mysteries of their identities. This is a liberating discovery, and it allows their autobiographies to testify to the truth of Stanley Kunitz's view that "our best songs are body-songs."[55]

54. Ibid., 59, 60. Gallop, *Thinking Through the Body*, 2.

55. Fiedler, *Freaks*, 20. Stanley Kunitz, *Next-to-Last Things: New Poems and Essays*, 53. Interestingly, the line is not from one of the former poet laureate's verses but from his essay "The Wisdom of the Body." The complete thought, which is the last sentence in the essay, reads: "Our most sublime thoughts have their feet planted in clay; our best songs are body-songs."

3

• • • • • • • • • • • **Magic**

The Performing Body

In those moments on a basketball court. . . . I feel the power of
imagination that creates a sense of mystery and wonder I last accepted in childhood, before the mind hardened.

~ *Bill Bradley*

ORMER BOSTON CELTIC BILL RUSSELL'S INTEREST IN MAGIC
began during his childhood in rural Louisiana when his mother
told him stories about "haints" and recounted a miraculous
event when he was a baby and dying from a malady that the doctors
could not diagnose. In his parents' desperation they turned to a nun
in the Catholic hospital where they had taken him, and she went to
the chapel and prayed about him until she had a vision. When she returned, she told his parents to hold the infant Russell by his ankles.
After a minute of dangling in the air, he coughed up a piece of corn-
bread that had lodged in his throat and over several days had caused
his body's defenses to drain all his strength fighting it. His mother interpreted the event as a sign that he was "charmed" and would carry
a special blessing in life.

For all his strong sense of logic and the intelligence he cultivated
as a student, Russell never lost his belief in magic, and he came to understand it as a concept that expressed an awareness of the mysteries of existence. "I still believe," he writes in his memoir, "that most

of what people really care about comes from the realm of magic—sex, religion, art, the spark in someone's personality."[1] It also played a role in the sport that he cared about so passionately, suddenly appearing in those rare but distinctive moments on the court that deserve to be called magic.

The most common sports term for these experiences is "peak performance." The phrase actually has some interesting connotations, but most people who use it do not consider its metaphoric implications and instead confine their ideas about it to clinical issues. They reduce it to a physiological sensation, but Russell clearly intends it to describe a more complex experience that conjures up something besides the merely physical, something that eludes the rule and line of mere reason. When he conceives of it as a spark that flares up in sexuality, artistic expression, personality, and religious feelings, he suggests a quasi-divine energy that I have compared to the Greek concept of the daimonic. I have also identified it as a vital energy that we associate with childhood, and Russell says about his experiences of magic that although people "think that their really important life will begin when they're an adult, ... many adults realize later that the important things in their lives happened when they were kids."[2]

The focal point of Russell's chapter is not a general argument about the presence of magic in life. He is more interested in the revelatory appearance of magic, the moment of experience when the body performs this magic. The chapter begins with an account of what he describes as a "mystical revelation" he had his junior year in high school. He credits the experience with the power to give the direction of his life a dramatic, right-angled turn. He believes it transformed his sense of who he was, changing his self-hatred as a black man into a warm confidence that he channeled into many areas of his life. It was clearly a conversion experience, a central trope in most traditional autobiographies going back to Augustine's *Confessions*. He conceptualizes it as a dramatic moment that freed him from his "old self," which had aimlessly gnawed on his failures, and that gave birth to a new view of himself and the world. "It was like waking up" is the way he describes the remarkable change that took place. It cast a spell on him. He remembers that "new skills seemed to drop down

1. Russell and Branch, *Second Wind*, 54–55.
2. Ibid., 54.

out of the sky, and I felt as if I had a new eye or had tapped a new compartment of my brain."[3] It was a moment of magic he never forgot. The subject of "The Echoing Green" focused on sports as a state of being, a feeling of freedom and spontaneity that we can attribute to the daimonic energy that keeps alive the eternal child within us, and "Body Songs" located the source of this feeling in the body. This chapter shifts the angle of perspective to reflect upon not the general state of being but athletes' remarkably similar accounts of their experiences of the specific moment, the particular vision, that occurs when the daimonic suddenly surfaces and creates a new understanding and a new world.

• The "Invisible Hand": Sports Performance as "Physical Genius"

Before looking at these moments of magic, it is helpful to reflect upon what makes the great athlete receptive to these experiences. Using the concept of the daimonic as a way of understanding sports challenges the stereotype of the "dumb jock." Conceptualizations of sports often place it on a spectrum that ranges from war to art, with the latter metaphor asking us to see sports as an act of self-expression and self-creation. To consider the extraordinary body of a great athlete as an instrument of performance is to credit the athlete with a gift and a kind of awareness that belie the demeaning stereotype. He or she possesses a special ability that can be thought of as "physical genius."

In a 1999 essay in the *New Yorker* entitled "The Physical Genius," Malcolm Gladwell, who later published the related book *Blink: The Power of Thinking without Thinking,* compares the extraordinary talents of surgeon Charlie Wilson, musician Yo-Yo Ma, and hockey player Wayne Gretzky. Charlie Wilson specializes in neurosurgery, a field generally thought to attract the best and the brightest physicians. Gladwell describes him in athletic terms. He is a "superstar" who performs "blindfolded acrobatics," and his "distinctive fluidity and grace" remind the author of Willie Mays. Brain surgery, like sports, is a dramatic life in extremis, as we learn when we think about Gladwell's description of aneurysm repair as "bomb disposal." What

3. Ibid., 51, 52, 54, 60.

Gretzky and cellist Yo-Yo Ma have in common with Wilson, Glad-well concludes, is "an affinity for translating thought into action."[4] It is this conception of physical genius that justifies viewing skilled surgeons as similar in some ways to athletes and respecting athletes as more than "dumb jocks." It also proposes that what kinesiologists call "peak performance" partakes of a kind of magic that cannot be explained in purely physiological terms.

On the other hand, the magic is not mere smoke and mirrors. It flows, in part, from the body. The surgeon, the artist, and the athlete all possess extraordinary coordination. The perfectly synchronized muscle actions they perform are governed by specific neurological mechanisms in the cerebellum and the basal ganglia. But, as we suspect, the talents of people like Wilson, Ma, and Gretzky extend far beyond their superior coordination.

Gladwell cites seven-time National League batting champion Tony Gwynn as an example in pointing to other factors that contribute to physical genius. He points out that a typical major-league fastball travels at 89 miles per hour and reaches the plate in about 460 milliseconds, and a hitter with a quick bat uses around 160 milliseconds in his swing. These two actions may seem to even out, but the third ingredient is that the batter must decide when to begin his swing, what particular stroke to use, and where to swing. These decisions typically take somewhere between 190 and 450 milliseconds for a great hitter like Gwynn. They also involve a variety of variables. What is the particular situation? Does Gwynn want to begin a rally and thus needs only a single, or are there two outs in the bottom of the ninth, his team trailing by a run with a runner on first, and a double or triple is required to drive the tying run home? What is the count, what pitch does this particular pitcher often throw to Gwynn in this situation, and what kind of swing is best to attack it? Gwynn was well known for the hours he spent reviewing videotapes of his encounters with opposing pitchers and he kept a statistical "book" on all of them, so in the milliseconds he had to act he was making a real decision from among several options. Clearly, IQ, not just a physical version of IQ, is a part of the process.[5]

---

4. Malcolm Gladwell, "Physical Genius," 57, 58.
5. Ibid., 58–59.

Gladwell proposes that this is what we mean when we talk about the "feel" great athletes have for the game or say that they "see" the court or the field in a special way. They may have great peripheral vision, but their "feel" has more to do with their ability to pick up on subtle patterns that other people do not recognize. In an interview Gladwell cites, Wayne Gretzky's description of hockey reinforces this thesis: "the whole sport is angles and caroms, forgetting the straight direction the puck is going, calculating where it will be diverted, factoring in all the interruptions." Surgeon Charlie Wilson's explanation is less precise than Gretzky's, but very similar in its implications. "Sometimes during the course of an operation, there'll be several possible ways of doing something," he says, "and I'll size them up and, without having any conscious reason, I'll just do one of them." His rare ability to slice immediately to just the right place in the cerebellum defies logical dissection. The physical genius this requires is something Wilson thinks of as "sort of an invisible hand."[6] Therein lies the magic.

But it is clear that a part of the mystery is pattern recognition. The geometric lines that Gretzky sees, as well as his anticipation of teammates who will suddenly appear in spaces that were until then empty ice, are patterns he grasps. Similarly, one of Wilson's colleagues explains that his ability to cut down to an aneurysm in a quarter of the time it takes other brain surgeons depends upon his awareness of the "gestalt" of the surgical field. His construction of a gestalt is also an example of pattern recognition. Gladwell adds that this aspect of physical genius is what psychologists call "chunking," the ability to store familiar sequences in long-term memory as a single unit, or chunk.[7] Chess masters, artists, athletes, and other geniuses of this kind are able to break down the board, the piece of musical composition, or the playing field into a handful of chunks that they have encountered before. As a result, they do not see individual units but clusters that have patterns. Wayne Gretzky, for example, summons up information from his bank account of knowledge—not just actual past games but videotapes he has studied—so that he sees not so much a set of moving players as a number

6. Ibid., 59.
7. Ibid., 62.

of situations.[8] Long before the actual pattern emerges, the athlete, as well as other gifted performers like Wilson and Ma, have also visualized over and over what they will do. This ability to translate thought into action is the essence of physical genius.

Not coincidentally, a kind of pattern recognition sometimes lies at the heart of visions, mysteries, and cults. Think of the sphinx that traditionally answers questions only with riddles. The sphinx does not "give" the answer or speak the answer in the usual sense of those phrases. The answer is *present* in the riddle, however, if the questioner can figure it out, that is, perceive the design or pattern underlying the riddle. The sphinx inhabits a world of magic, but a crucial meaning of its mysteries is that the answer must be found within the person whose quest has led to its "inner" sanctum. Or consider the implications of traditional myths and legends about the wisdom of the sibyl. She answers from her cave with a wind that blows out leaves that the quester must "read" by finding a pattern in them. Modern-day fortune tellers who read our futures in the tea leaves lack real magic because it is only we who have the power to see the gestalt of our lives in the patterns of the leaves. That is the true magic. Stories about sphinxes and sibyls, like the concept of chunking, neither explain nor explain away the magic, however. Instead, as fables, they image forth what we somehow know because of our "inner eye," or what the tactile genius calls "the invisible hand."

Tony Gwynn's encyclopedic library of tapes that he laboriously watched and the "book" he kept on each pitcher imply that the magic is "within" in another respect as well. Despite our assumption that great athletes are usually "natural athletes," Tony Gwynn and others of his caliber exercise an exhaustive and meticulous preparation. They may not be natural athletes, but it is in their nature to devote themselves to their sports. Like most successful people, they are driven, often compulsively striving for perfection. Former Boston Red Sox baseball player Ted Williams claims in his autobiography that, even blindfolded, he could pick out the one bat of the six bats in front of him that was a half ounce heavier than the others. He was also sensitive to the slight changes in a bat's weight caused by the moisture present in the early part of the season when the weather in Boston was still cold and damp some evenings.

8. Ibid., 63.

• Acts of Imagination: Translating Thought into Performance

What the examples of Gwynn and Williams suggest is that physical genius involves more than technical skills or intelligence. It also requires the right kind of attitude and personality. Williams was obsessed with hitting and with his bats, even to the extent of taking them to the post office to have them weighed in the years before the Red Sox bought a scale for the locker room. His special "feel" for the game was literally reflected in his handling of his bats, but in this case it is clear that his attitude—his passion for hitting and his insistence on perfection—was a far more important factor than a physical gift such as his wonderful twenty-ten vision. Magic occurs when, in the current parlance of sports, the athlete is "in the zone." But reaching this peak of performance takes hours and hours of repeating the same physical movement. Why else would Larry Bird write in his autobiography, appropriately entitled *Drive*, that in high school he got up early every day and by 6 a.m. began his routine of shooting at least 200 free throws before school started? The magic has to be "within" in this sense, too.

It seems obvious that physical genius cannot be traced to a single gene or factor. It is much more than the sum of its parts. Gladwell singles out a final factor that helps to constitute physical genius—the imagination. It is, I think, the most important and the most elusive of the factors, and it recapitulates in itself the dynamic that makes the whole greater than its individual components. As Bartlett Giamatti argues in his reflections on the meaning of leisure and play, sports is a performance in which the athlete takes the vision in his or her head and makes it palpable with the body.[9] The athlete translates thought into performance.

To understand the imaginative nature of sports performance, it is helpful to consider further what we mean by imagination. In the eighteenth century rationalists proposed a faculty psychology that conceived of the mind as composed of various faculties or "compartments," each responsible for its own particular mental function. In this model of the mind, the imagination occupied a single compartment and consisted of a storehouse for images we used when-

9. Giamatti, *Take Time for Paradise*, 40.

ever we wrote or spoke—in the famous definition of wit offered by the leading poet of that era, Alexander Pope—"What oft was *Thought*, but ne'er so well *Exprest.*"[10] In the nineteenth century, however, organicism replaced Newtonian physics as the ruling scientific model, and, accordingly, faculty psychology's mechanical view of the imagination was superseded by the new Romantic concept, which pictured the imagination as a total working of the mind that involved thought, feeling, memory, and intuition.

In contrast to John Locke's older view of the mind as a tabula rasa, a blank slate, which passively accepted sensory impressions and formed generalizations based upon them, the nineteenth-century writers attributed to the human mind the power actually to transform the world it saw. We might think of this inner power as analogous to what medieval alchemists sought in their efforts to transform base metals into gold, and remember that one person's science may be another's magic. In Romanticism's rebellion against the increasingly rigid claims of reason and common sense, the concept of the imagination represented a resurgence of the claims of a kind of magic, but in this instance a magic within. The Romantic imagination was also part of a rediscovery of the power of childhood, of folk literature, and of the supernatural. What linked these subjects was the belief that the supernatural or the marvelous was always latent in the commonplace if we could only respond to it in the spirit of spontaneous free play.

Although these abstract generalizations about the evolution of culture may seem far removed from the daily round of sporting events, they serve to remind us once again that all human activities, no matter how ordinary they seem, are expressions of a larger cultural construction. In this case, the modern understanding of sports reflects our culture's view that the interaction of the body and the mind in play is animated by an act of imagination, a concept we may conceive as representing the continuing presence of magic in the world. Athletes exercise their imaginations, first of all, in the technique of visualization. Their training often includes a "virtual rehearsal" for the sporting contest in which they imagine what is going to happen. But because of the joy that releases their imaginations and the resulting

10. Alexander Pope, *Pastoral Poetry and An Essay on Criticism*, 273. The line is from *An Essay on Criticism*.

joy that flows from their imaginative acts, sometimes a moment of magic is created that transcends mere technique. Some of the most interesting accounts in sports autobiographies center on these experiences of magic.

Bill Russell's insights in *Second Wind* are very similar to a number of the ideas Gladwell discusses. Russell in effect created himself as a basketball player through acts of imagination. He was a sickly child afflicted by a series of medical emergencies and grew up to be "the classic ninety-pound weakling." At six foot five and 140 pounds in the eleventh grade, he had, he confesses, the physique of a nail. Certainly, there was no discernible magic in his body at that time. "When I opened a soup can," he says about his clumsy body, "it felt as if I was trying to take apart a watch with a sledgehammer."[11] Even when he managed to start on the basketball team his senior year, he was at best a mediocre player. There were only six teams in his school's league and the newspapers selected a first team all-league team, a second team all-league team, and a third team all-league team, but Russell failed to make any of these teams or even the long list of honorable mentions. He assumed he was headed for a blue-collar job at the San Francisco Naval Shipyards after graduation, not for a college basketball scholarship, let alone the NBA Hall of Fame. Through a series of lucky coincidences, however, he was asked to join a touring team of high school players, and during those crucial weeks he became an outstanding player by imagining himself as one.

More specifically, he used the technique of visualization to do what the star players on the team were already able to do. The technique itself was not new to him. In junior high school he had wanted to be an architect, and he tried to prepare himself by studying the paintings of Michelangelo and da Vinci, memorizing every detail and then trying to draw re-creations of them from memory. He thought he could transfer this ability to architecture: "I wanted to conceive of a building in my mind and then make it reality."[12]

While he did not realize his dream of becoming an architect, in *Second Wind* he discusses the way he was able to transfer this method to basketball. He first studied the moves of the team's best player, and then on the long bus rides to the site of the next game he would draw

11. Russell and Branch, *Second Wind*, 52.
12. Ibid., 67.

"mental blueprints" or "create an instant replay on the inside of [his] eyelids." He practiced his new moves over and over, but first he visualized them: "the movies I saw in my head seemed to have their own projector, and whenever I closed my eyes it would run." Gradually, his memory bank contained not only individual moves but larger clusters. He would imagine himself as the mirror image of the star rather than the star himself, and then he expanded the "two-man show" in his mind and sketched out whole scenes of the two of them in action on the court. This sounds like the first stage in the development of the "chunking" that Gladwell discusses. As Russell notes, "I got the details right, and repeatedly they fell into place," and later he "began to daydream about sequences of moves instead of individual ones." Certainly, he discovered the essence of physical genius when in such "dreams" imitation was replaced by imagination: "I didn't copy them [his new moves]; I invented them. They grew out of my imagination."[13]

The result of his imagination is magic. "I could barely contain myself," he writes about the joy he felt because of his early successes in translating his imagination into physical action. "I was so elated I thought I'd float right out of the gym." He says that in his later career he lived for such special "spells," as he calls them. They were "magical" and gave him a "mystical feeling." They warrant being described as mystical for Russell because of the feeling of transcendence he experienced. He writes in *Second Wind* that in some games he was caught up in a spell that encompassed the entire court, not just him. He says that there is a force that "surrounds" everyone on the court. He insists that, for the magic to happen, it must take over the play of his team, the opposing team, and even the performance of the referees: "The feeling would spread to the other guys, and we'd all levitate."[14]

His description of what happens in such a game captures several of the features that Gladwell analyzes:

> The game would be in a white heat of competition, and yet somehow I wouldn't feel competitive—which is a miracle in itself. I'd be . . . straining, coughing up parts of my lungs as we ran, and yet I never felt the pain. The game would move so quickly that every fake, cut and

13. Ibid., 68, 66, 68, 84, 70.
14. Ibid., 67, 155, 156.

pass would be surprising, and yet nothing could surprise me. It was almost as if we were playing in slow motion. During those spells I could almost sense how the next play would develop and where the next shot would be taken. Even before the other team brought the ball in bounds, I could feel it so keenly that I'd want to shout to my team-mates, "It's coming there!"—except that I knew everything would change if I did. My premonitions would be consistently correct, and I always felt then that I not only knew all the Celtics by heart but also all the opposing players, and that they all knew me. There have been many times in my career when I felt moved or joyful, but these were the moments when I had chills pulsing up and down my spine.[15]

Like the various components of physical genius, this moment of magic is suspended between the rational and the intuitive, between the physical and the imaginative, between the burst of speed on the fast break and the sensation that time itself is almost stopped. On the one hand, his "premonition" can be explained by his mastery of "chunking" as he anticipates the geometric lines of the next play and the next shot, but, on the other hand, the premonition is a product of the "miracle" that is taking place somewhere beyond the conscious wills of Russell and the other players. Russell was one of the fiercest competitors in the game, but he confesses that on those rare occasions when the spell lasted until the end of the game he felt so elevated that he did not care whether his team had won or lost. His capacity to feel this kind of magic helps explain why villagers who saw him perform in clinics he conducted in Africa used a word for him that translates to "magician."[16]

- **"Before the Mind Hardened": Sports Performance and the Transcendent Moment**

Bill Bradley, who many people do not know was a professional basketball player for the New York Knicks before he became a U.S. senator, records in a diary he kept during his playing days his thoughts about these special moments. He prefaces his description by remarking that usually certain conditions are necessary if the magic is

15. Ibid., 156–57.
16. Ibid., 90.

to occur. He observes that, however strong his love of the game, the modern athlete cannot escape very divided aims. He wants to play well and to win, but he also wants to make as much money as possible and enjoys the adulation of the fans that washes over him during the contest. While he cannot will these magical moments, they are far more likely to happen if the night is one in which he momentarily forgets these other pulls on his consciousness. He characterizes the experience as one of wholeness of body and mind, but this state requires that the athlete must do his part. He cannot enter the "zone" if part of him is somewhere else. What happens next, Bradley writes, is powerful, but simple and pure.

Bradley tries to put into words something that is almost beyond the reach of words:

> . . . it is far more than a passing emotion. It is as if a lightning bolt strikes, bringing insight into an uncharted area of human experience. It makes perfect sense at the same time it seems new and undiscovered. . . . no one else but me can feel what it all means. . . . No one else can sense the inexorable rightness of the moment. . . . I sense an immediate transporting enthusiasm and a feeling that everything is in perfect balance.[17]

Bradley's experience is one of magic, but it is not identical to Russell's. Russell feels a sense of wholeness, but for him it is created by a harmonious union of everyone on the court. They are all caught up in the "white heat" of the moment. Bradley's experience is private. As he explains earlier in this section of the diary, the "experience is one of beautiful isolation."[18] The mystery that surrounds Russell is the mystery inherent in life in those moments when we are open enough to catch it. The mystery Bradley discovers is, he says, "an uncharted area of human experience." The mystery lies within himself, in an understanding of his deeper self. And if Russell emphasizes the diffused "white heat" all around him, the moment is concentered for Bradley in the flash of a single "lightning bolt." The lightning strike heralds a kind of epiphany. For Bradley, the significance of the moment lies in the insight it brings, as opposed to the warmth of feeling it brings to Russell. The moment hits him like the answer to the riddle of the sphinx or the

17. Bradley, *Life on the Run,* 221.
18. Ibid.

prophecy of the sibyl: "It makes perfect sense at the same time it seems new and undiscovered." The quasi-religious and visionary qualities of the experience are suggested when he calls it "transporting." It is a moment of immortality in the sense that life rises above itself, offering a transcendent understanding of who and what we are.

Bradley concludes the passage with some psychological reflections on this kind of magic. Like the poet Wordsworth, who called such epiphanies "spots of time," Bradley argues, in effect, that "The child is father of the Man."[19] He traces his ability to get caught up in the magic to childhood:

> Those moments require a childlike imagination. In those moments on a basketball court I feel as a child and know as an adult. . . . I feel the power of imagination that creates a sense of mystery and wonder I last accepted in childhood, before the mind hardened.[20]

Whatever their differences, Bradley, like Russell, finds in these moments a point of confluence between sports, art, and religion. When he speaks of the "sense of mystery and wonder," he describes a feeling of awe that is clearly quasi-religious in nature. He also likens the experience to art and vision when he says that it "requires a childlike imagination." What Bradley wants to emphasize is that sports can be a way of seeing and a way of creating the self. Like Russell, he identifies the experience with something that is more than the peak performance of the body. Actually, Bradley does not distinguish the body from the workings of the larger self. He associates the transcendent moment with childhood because of its lack of self-consciousness. For the child, thought and feeling have not yet been divorced. The child has not yet been taught that the body and the soul or mind or imagination are separate compartments in our lives. The magic that Bradley discovers in the transcendent moment is that he is and can continue to be the child he once was.

19. Wordsworth, *The Poetical Works of Wordsworth*, 210, 277. The first phrase, which is a touchstone indelibly associated with Wordsworth, is from Book 12 of the 1850 version of *The Prelude*. As previously cited, the other line is from "My Heart Leaps Up."
20. Bradley, *Life on the Run*, 221.

Bradley is, at least in moments like this, what Christian K. Messenger calls a "ritual hero," an athlete who participates in sports not for utilitarian ends but for the pure joy of creative self-expression.[21] As Bradley puts it, "The money and the championships are reasons I play, but what I'm addicted to are the nights like tonight when something special happens on the court." An anecdote he recounts earlier in the book reinforces why he loves the game so much. At a party at a friend's apartment in Chicago, another guest asked him if he really liked playing basketball, and when Bradley replied that he enjoyed it more than anything else he could be doing at that stage of his life, the guest said he thought he understood how he felt. He explained that in college he played the trumpet in a band and had a chance to go on tour and make a record, but his father had persuaded him to go to law school because of the lack of security in a musical career. When Bradley asked him if he liked the law, his response was, "It's okay, but nothing like playing the trumpet."[22] The story takes us back to Bradley's quotation from Fitzgerald's "Ring." Whatever its flaws, there is a magic about sports, and Bradley, like Ring, knows he "could find nothing finer."

• "Night Dreams": The Zone of Reverie

The accounts in Russell and Bradley's autobiographies single out the features of these special moments that are typically found in other athletes' descriptions of them: the heightened senses, the winding down of time, often the feeling of being outside the body watching themselves, and the clarity of vision. The combined effect creates an experience of transcendence. The sweaty toiler who has prepared himself for the game with countless repetitions in practice suddenly is transformed into an artist. Tennis player Tracy Austin points out that the ball appears to be much bigger than normal—something baseball players also commonly report—and adds that "everything seems quiet and peaceful, it seems like you're playing in a tunnel." Often, this concentering of the lines of sight is a prelude to a countermovement upward and outward. Sprinter Lynda Huey describes it as a "beyondness," the special place her body takes her when the

21. Messenger, *Sport and the Spirit of Play in American Fiction,* 8, 12, 231–37.
22. Bradley, *Life on the Run,* 220–21, 46.

fatigue of running with its mixture of pain and pleasure pushes her deeper into herself than normal consciousness allows. Bullfighter Patricia McCormick uses images that capture the same intensity of focus that then releases an opposing sensation of expansion. "I forget everything but that bull," she writes in *Lady Bullfighter*, "and the movements come naturally and instinctively while something inside me swells, like the bursting open of doors and windows of a room that has been suffocatingly close."[23]

Michael Oriard relates that the first time he experienced this kind of magic he was in the sixth grade and was "stunned" by his miraculous catch of a long pass. The catch was not lucky, he claims, because he had *known* he was going to catch it even though he never saw it in flight. "Without seeing it. But knowing it," is the only way he can try to describe the "mystery in which I had participated." The picture of his arms extended fully to grasp a football he cannot see makes concrete the "stretch of freedom" McCormick and other athletes testify they also experience in these moments.[24] As Bradley puts it, once "the mind hardens," most people develop along with their other cautious protections a fear of flying. But not the athlete who is an eternal child.

Consider, as a summary of what so many athletes feel, basketball star Spencer Haywood's attempt to put the magic into words:

> I was flying. I was an eagle. . . . I was walking on air. . . . I really felt at times I was weightless. I was in a twilight zone. Sometimes I was almost a spectator at my own show, looking down and seeing myself doing these things, as if somebody else was using my body while I hovered like a cloud and watched.[25]

Diana Nyad's *Other Shores* includes a chapter about an intriguing variation on this subject. Nyad is currently a radio and television sports broadcaster, but in the 1970s she was the women's world marathon swimming champion. She at one time held the speed record for the twenty-eight-mile swim around Manhattan island, and in addition to her races in warm climates she swam a fifteen-mile course across Lake Ontario in forty-degree waters and with the

23. Austin and Brennan, *Beyond Center Court*, 91. Huey, *A Running Start*, 60. McCormick, *Lady Bullfighter: The Autobiography of the North American Matador*, 17.
24. Oriard, *The End of Autumn*, 20, 21. McCormick, *Lady Bullfighter*, 17.
25. Haywood and Osler, *Spencer Haywood*, 135.

strong currents of the Niagara River to fight. And she once lost twenty-four pounds during a forty-hour swim in the North Sea. In her autobiography she mentions that she needed either hospitalization or medical attention after all but one of her marathon swims. In 1979 Nyad stroked her way to the longest swim in history, both for men and women. The distance was 102.5 miles—from the island of Bimini to the Florida shore—a record that still stands more than twenty-five years later.

It is not hard to understand why marathon swimming is considered an "extreme sport." Nyad was attracted to what she thought of as the sport's "primeval conflict." She saw it as an effort to conquer geographical space with no aid or equipment other than the human body and will. In her autobiography she describes it as a battle for survival against a brutal, indefatigable foe—the sea—and the only victory possible, she says, is to "touch the other shore."[26] The only other sports besides marathon running that she compares her swimming to are boxing and even more primitive hand-to-hand combat. She insists, however, that the ultimate foe lies within. Extreme sports usually represent the athlete's refusal to accept limits, and Nyad used her strength and her denial of pain to construct her marathon swims as what she conceptualizes in *Other Shores* as a test of her integrity against the threats posed by fear, doubt, and boredom. Because of her brutal training regimen and the spirit required for the swims, her self-image is that of a Spartan warrior.

Because she is a self-confessed extremist who competed in an extreme sport, the form of magic she discusses in *Other Shores* is extraordinary, if not somewhat bizarre. What conjures up the magic is the sensory deprivation marathon swimmers experience. Unlike what happens in other sports, the sensory deprivation in marathon swimming is almost absolute. Nyad participated in scientific experiments of sensory deprivation in which she floated in an isolation tank, but she claims that marathon swimming magnifies a hundredfold the effect created by the tank and that the physical exhaustion during a race adds even more to the effect. She had to wear goggles to protect her eyes, and within a few minutes after the start of a swim they fogged over and after about ten hours she became almost completely blind. She wore four caps for warmth, and her hearing was 90 percent ineffectual. Her

26. Nyad, *Other Shores,* 152.

crew communicated with her by blowing a police whistle, but they usually had to blow it twelve or more times before it broke through into her consciousness. Once, her trainer set up giant speakers to blast music to ease her boredom. After a few hours the crew almost went crazy from the noise, but she never heard a note. The other senses also failed. Her sense of touch was distorted by the immersion time, and taste and smell were obliterated in the water. She became so locked in the worlds of water and herself that there was no communication with her crew and no penetration by outside stimuli.

What happened after hours of sensory deprivation reflects the unique powers of physical genius. She explains the "night dreams" she experienced in several different ways. On the one hand, she recognizes that the experience is a form of self-hypnosis. She says her superior, pinpoint focus released her mind to travel, remember, and imagine. She cites the founder of the Esalen Institute who once said that sports is a Western yoga. She had also practiced Eastern meditation, and she says her dreams were similar to that state of mind. "When you have reached your core, and outside stimuli can't penetrate," she writes, "your mind and your spirit leave your body on a free adventure."[27] In some of these spells she was able to go far back into her childhood, as early as when she was only two years old, and sift through the events again and reinterpret the dialogue that took place at the time.

But the analogy of yoga or meditation accounts for only certain aspects of these experiences. The peace she felt had its counterpart in a joy that lifted her up, a "mental exhilaration" she calls it.[28] She saw wild fantasies and painted scenes on her eyelids. She compares these visions to the trances induced by LSD, a hallucinogen that she also took as a point of comparison in her studies about sensory deprivation and brain activity. These bizarre "trips" and the fantasies they unleashed could also take on a nightmarish character. During one long swim off the coast of Argentina she thought she was being attacked by a pack of seagulls and imagined the birds' beaks gouging her head and blood gushing from her face into her eyes. It was a scene out of Alfred Hitchcock's *The Birds*, she remembers, and the fantasy lasted for more than half an hour.

27. Ibid., 103, 105.
28. Ibid., 110.

Such horrors were rare, however, and the real danger was that if she let herself go too deeply into the visions she saw she would not be able to swim the race. She did not want to block the "mind expansion," but she did not want it to diminish the effectiveness of her swimming. She had to keep up her stroke count and rhythm, and she had to swim straight ahead rather than get lost in circles. This required that she engage another part of the brain in addition to her imagination. Her technique was to use counting games. She sang "Row, Row, Row Your Boat" 150 times, followed by 25 rounds of "Frère Jacques" in sets of French, German, and English. She synchronized the songs with her strokes and she knew how many constituted the interval of an hour. The counting game accomplished two different effects. First, it acted as a self-hypnosis device that placed the body on "automatic pilot" and let her mind travel into the world of fantasy. At the same time, she writes, it attached her "inner voice" or consciousness to some intelligible, objective-world symbols so that she did not slip completely into the beyond.[29]

She again conceptualizes this state of mind in two different ways, one rather clinical, the other suggestive of the world of magic. She had read various studies about the brain, especially those that begin with the fact that we typically use only 12 percent of the brain's capacity and that discuss the relationship between activities governed by the right hemisphere of the brain and those governed by the left. Her conclusion is that in her marathons the result of the sensory deprivation was that her mind hovered "somewhere in limbo between the absolute concrete world of conscious thought and the seemingly uncontrollable state of illogical fantasy." She also conceptualizes it in a way that is less scientifically based as "float[ing] in limbo between the unbearable sanity of knowing the exact extent of the pain I am feeling and the glorious insanity of zooming away on a wild, safe LSD trip."[30]

Her images are suggestive. The "glorious insanity" sounds somewhat like the "fine madness" that we identify with poetry and poetic inspiration. The concept is as old as the ancient Greek notion of the "furor" that possessed the poet in the act of creation. Similarly, she locates the world she entered in these experiences as a "limbo." Taken

29. Ibid., 112, 113.
30. Ibid., 118, 113.

together with her overall characterization of the experience as a "night dream," the state of mind seems remarkably like what nineteenth-century poets called reverie. Reverie is a kind of limbo, a border zone between ordinary waking consciousness and sleep or dream. The mind is awake, but the usual control of reason and logic is relaxed, allowing other aspects of the psyche such as imagination and instinct to come into fuller play. Reverie makes it possible for the appearance of what Charlie Wilson calls "the invisible hand." Nyad points out that in the sensory deprivation experiments in the tank, as in her swims, the "brain didn't go to sleep; when . . . 'left in peace' . . . , the brain is vitally active." This is like poetic reverie, and the results for Nyad were similar to those the poets experienced. She found the magic of "phenomenal mind expansion," and she says her best races were those in which her fantasies were rich, intense, and long-lasting.[31]

Although Diana Nyad's experiences are bizarre, they capture the essence of the magic moment in sports. She makes it clear that sports is particularly conducive to such moments, if the athlete is open and willing. Her realization that her fantasies were possible because the right and left sides of her brain "operate[d] simultaneously" also confirms Bill Bradley's notion about the wholeness of being that athletes achieve in these moments and that also makes the moments possible. Like Bradley, she also sees these experiences as transcendent ones. The athlete's laserlike focus allows the body to "act freely and intuitively as you have devotedly taught it, without interference from the conscious mind," and the sensation that follows is like "zooming away."[32] The magic lies in the transcendence of ordinary consciousness, something the rest of us understand only from afar as we remember the unself-conscious joys of childhood or the magic religion once wielded in earlier societies.

Nyad and Bradley also single out the sense of freedom that animates the movement. Bradley rid himself of business and personal distractions and discovered the freedom of a child before the mind hardens. Nyad found the imaginative freedom created by the literal freedom from external stimulus. With no demands or attachments, they could enjoy the free play of mind that is the essence of sports as an autotelic activity. Both Bradley and Nyad imply that the effect of the magic is

31. Ibid., 105, 118.
32. Ibid., 118, 111–12, 113.

that they lost themselves in order to find themselves. When the lightning bolt struck, Bradley forgot what T. S. Eliot calls "the profit and loss,"[33] and Nyad's sensory deprivation functioned like a surrender to another power— the rich and seething waters of the unconscious that are an analogue to the sea she swims. The act unlocked what she calls "a hallucination beyond my control." This description reinforces Bill Russell's assertion that what happens is "mystical." This loss of self, however, is a prelude to a discovery of a deeper and truer self. Nyad reached her "core" of being, and the magical effect of one swim, a single day, was that it was "like spending six months on a shrink's couch." She claims that "each marathon swim seems to make you psychologically a decade older." Because of this remarkable kind of "thinking through the body," she "remembered so much and imagined so much and discovered so much about [her]self and others."[34]

The immediate after-effect of Nyad's experiences was more physical and spiritual than intellectual, however. In contrast to the joyful exhilaration of zooming away on the wings of fantasy, at the end of the swim she felt a sensation of security and tranquillity. Her mind, she says, was at rest. This, too, follows the pattern of the poetic reverie. Consider the striking parallels between Nyad's discussion of her experiences and the images she uses and the following passage from William Wordsworth's "Tintern Abbey" in which he tries to put into words his understanding of a reverie:

> . . . that blessed mood,
> In which the burthen of the mystery,
> In which the heavy and the weary weight
> Of all this unintelligible world,
> Is lightened:—that serene and blessed mood,
> In which the affections gently lead us on,—
> Until, the breath of this corporeal frame
> And even the motion of our human blood
> Almost suspended, we are laid asleep
> In body, and become a living soul;
> While with an eye made quiet by the power

33. T. S. Eliot, *The Complete Poems and Plays, 1909–1950,* 46. The line is from the "Death by Water" section of *The Waste Land:* "Phlebas the Phoenician, a fortnight dead, / Forgot the cry of gulls, and the deep sea swell / And the profit and loss."
34. Nyad, *Other Shores,* 105, 114.

Of harmony, and the deep power of joy,
We see into the life of things. (37–49)[35]

The ability to focus on joy so intensely that for a moment we are lifted above our ordinary selves and the mundane world and experience a deep peace and a clear vision—that is magic. It is the magic of the poet, the dreamer, the lover, the child, and, sometimes, the athlete. In defining the concept of "sacred time" in sports, Michael Novak argues that freedom from the restraints of ordinary time allows the athlete to achieve a sort of immortality, not in the sense of living forever or being remembered by others forever, "but because it is a deed not always given to mortals."[36]

Despite all the economic and social problems that afflict contemporary sports, the opportunity to witness moments of magic is one of the reasons fans return to the ballpark for the next home stand or read the sports pages first in the morning. It is magical to see an image of the free and whole person they wish to be. That is the self-image that many athletes present in their autobiographies. They describe transcendent experiences that imply that to achieve self-knowledge they acted in fidelity to the deep nature within them—that they expressed the daimonic within them as their bodies performed magic. Their descriptions of the transcendent moment also suggest "To enter the kingdom of heaven, ye must become as a little child." Their feelings define them as creatures subject not only to the law of history but also to the law of eternity. Extraordinary athletes like Bill Russell, Bill Bradley, and Diana Nyad know that self-knowledge is in part to be found in the external events of their lives but that a fuller and deeper sense of who they are lies in those infrequent moments of magic. Although their autobiographies celebrate their tangible achievements, some of the most memorable passages explore those transcendent experiences that led them to the very mysteries of identity itself.

---

35. Wordsworth, *The Poetical Works*, 91–93. Although the poem is always referred to by the shorthand title "Tintern Abbey," Wordsworth titled the poem "Lines Composed a Few Miles above Tintern Abbey, on Revisiting the Banks of the Wye during a Tour, July 13, 1798."

36. Novak, "American Sports, American Virtues," 37. Novak also devotes a chapter section to the subject of "sacred time" in *The Joy of Sports: End Zones, Bases, Baskets, Balls, and the Consecration of the American Spirit,* 126–31.

4

• • • • • • • • **The End of Autumn**

When you're no longer an NFL player, . . . You no longer have a purpose. You wake up and wonder why you should even get out of bed.
What are you supposed to do with the rest of your life—play Nintendo?

~former Green Bay Packer Ken Ruettgers

I'm throwing twice as hard as I used to, but the ball isn't going
as fast.

~ Lefty Gomez

IN *PASSING SHOTS* TENNIS PLAYER PAM SHRIVER REGISTERS A FEAR
that haunts most of us:

> My fear is the fear of retirement. I've seen too many people stumble on
> their way to retirement. I don't want to stumble. I want to leave when
> I choose, not when my game or my body takes the choice out of my
> hands. I don't want to grow dependent on the applause or the atten-
> tion or the high of winning. . . . I'm beginning to think how more than
> half of my career is already over.[1]

Shriver's situation is very different from ours, however, in one crucial
aspect: when she wrote this, she was only twenty-two years old. At
the age when other professionals have reached only the first stage of

---

1. Shriver, Deford, and Adams, *Passing Shots,* 132, 134.

their careers, most athletes are ending their careers. They must retire, that is, if injuries have not already forced a premature departure from their sport. Even athletes who avoid or survive serious injuries rarely play professionally beyond their early to mid-thirties. How strange it is to see how young these "aging veterans," as they are usually called, look when they remove their caps or helmets.

Their situation is much more complicated than that of other workers who make several career shifts during their lives. There is much more at stake in leaving sports. "Retirement" is usually a euphemism because most players are forced to leave the game. In the parlance of team sports, they are "cut." The image is appropriate because they are usually injured or wounded in the process. Or, if we think of the conventional concept of the team as a "family" or social unit, they are "cut" in the sense of summarily dismissed, treated as if they never were. In football, the phrase often used is "a visit from the Turk." During training camp, "the Turk"—a ball boy or some other messenger— mysteriously appears during the afternoon or evening to summon the player and tell him to bring his playbook. The latter is the undeniable sign that he will not be coming back, except to pack and leave the camp as quietly and invisibly as possible. Most players live in fear of "the Turk."

Getting cut may mean that the player was not good enough to make the team, but in this age of salary caps and economically stressed teams playing in small-market cities, it may also mean that a talented veteran is being replaced by a less talented rookie with a much lower salary. How can a player really prepare for the inevitable when it is not always clear when that time has arrived? Even more to be feared than the new economic realities of sports is the sudden, career-ending injury. The "blown-out" knee, the fifth concussion in a period of only a few years, the dangerously enlarged heart just discovered after a spell of dizziness, the spinal hemorrhaging after a tackle that was executed exactly as always but this time resulted in a numbness in the legs—players can only fear, not prepare, for these all-too-frequent realities.

• "The Winter of Our Discontent"

The title of Roger Kahn's book about the Brooklyn Dodgers of the 1940s and 1950s, *The Boys of Summer,* and my chapter, "The Echoing

Green," select images that tie the lives of athletes to the seasons, but the images serve a double purpose. They capture the youth and innocence that athletes keep alive by playing sports, but they also foreshadow what is to come.[2] If the athlete, like the child, the lover, the dreamer, and the poet, is uniquely blessed in certain ways, his ultimate fate is unique in troubling ways. The fierceness of the competition for the very limited number of places on a team and the ever-present vulnerability to incapacitating injuries give a sense of impermanence and fragility to professional sports. It is not surprising, then, that this ethos would deepen to the point that most athletes see the end of their playing days as a kind of death. The common litany in sports autobiographies is that the players' "days are numbered," that "time is running out" for them, or that their "time has come." More than conveying the sense of impending death, this kind of language suggests that it is almost as if a sentence has been imposed upon them. But they are most disturbed by the untimeliness of the coming "death." It is premature, an unnatural acceleration of the life cycle. The end of autumn suddenly darkens the echoing green, as if a season of their lives had somehow been elided.

Reggie Jackson, the "Mr. October" of some of the New York Yankee World Series championship teams in the late 1970s, reflects upon the end of his career in his autobiography:

> It's like dying: nobody dies at the right time. Everybody feels, "If I just could've done that one more thing!" Your career is the same way. It doesn't end the way you want it to. It just ends.[3]

Pat Jordan, the writer who failed to reach the major leagues in his aborted career, feels the same way about his life in baseball: "it never seemed to end properly, neatly, all those bits and pieces finally forming some harmonious design. It just stopped, unfinished in my

2. I have used as the title for this chapter the title of Michael Oriard's autobiography. Oriard also reflects upon the relationship between the cycle of the seasons and the career of an athlete, and I am indebted to him for the general concept of this chapter in addition to the specific ideas in his book that I cite. The title essay in Pat Jordan's book *After the Sundown* is also concerned with this theme.

3. Jackson and Lupica, *Reggie*, 127.

memory, fragmented, so many pieces missing."[4] The problem is that
the story stops rather than concludes. A symbolic "death" comes for
the athlete long before his life as a whole is over. Like the novelist
Bernard Malamud, we may celebrate all the young Roy Hobbses as
"The Natural," but this kind of end is very unnatural. Ted Williams
hit a home run in his last time at bat and Michael Jordan's last shot
before retiring from the Chicago Bulls was a jumper in the final sec-
onds that won another NBA championship, but Reggie Jackson is
right. For most athletes, the career does not end in storybook fashion. It just ends, and in this story the hero "dies." That is the fate of
warriors. Former tennis champion Billie Jean King conceptualizes
sports in this way in her autobiography when she summarizes the
arc of an athlete's career: "You take scalps on the way up and lose
your own on the way down."[5]

• The Fate of Warriors

If the athlete has played for many years, particularly if most of his career was spent with the same team, we often find in the autobiography the refrain of *ubi sunt*. This motif means "Where are they now?"
and it is a literary convention that goes back to the classical ages and
also appears in Anglo-Saxon poetry. It is the lament of the warrior at
the end of an era. After a life of warfare, he looks around and discovers that he is almost the only one left. *Ubi sunt* is the elegiac cry
that echoes hollowly out of the mists of autumn. Whitey Ford, the
dominant pitcher on the great Yankee teams of the 1950s and 1960s,
ends his autobiography *Slick* with a commentary on the end of the
Yankee dynasty. The problem was that "everybody got old at once,"
and management had to compensate by making a series of trades,
"breaking up the Yankees gang and the Yankee spirit." His teammate
Mickey Mantle recounts in *The Mick* that he realized as he scanned
the locker room that "Only Whitey and I were left," and he repeats
Ford's lament: "The old days were gone." The two stars of the Milwaukee Braves' World Series years, Hank Aaron and Eddie Math-

4. Jordan, *A False Spring*, 11.
5. King and Deford, *Billie Jean*, 1.

ews, faced the same situation when they were the only players left from those winning teams. Mathews confesses in his autobiography, "I was starting to feel like a stranger on my own ballclub," and Aaron experienced the same unnatural feeling: "So many of my old friends and teammates had been sent away that I felt cut off from my past and out of place, almost like my class had graduated and I was still sitting at my desk as the new kids arrived in the fall."[6]

The sense of estrangement signals the passing of an era. In *Stranger to the Game*, Bob Gibson, the star pitcher of the St. Louis Cardinals, comments on the end of his career when only he and outfielder Lou Brock were left from the team that had won the pennant only a few years earlier. It is almost as if he had awakened from a time warp:

> The league was different, the fields were different, the rules were different, and most of all the names and faces were different. In the space of a single presidential term, we had moved into an all-new era that was a world removed from the one in which Cepeda had danced on the money trunk and Denny McLain and I had squared off in the World Series.[7]

Willie Mays found himself in a similar situation at the end of his career. When he retired, of the people who had played in the old Negro League, only Hank Aaron was still in baseball. Like Gibson, Mays also experienced the dramatic passage of time. "Suddenly," he writes in *Say Hey*, "I had become the old man of the Giants. . . . It seemed like only yesterday I was a teenager, with the great Joe DiMaggio as my idol."[8] Mays may have had to pinch himself, but only in sports was he an old man. When he became the senior citizen on the Giants, he was thirty-one years old. Boxing champ Jack Dempsey was jolted when he saw he was almost the only great star of the Golden Age of sports still active. "Ruth had been on the rise at the same time I had been," he reflects in his autobiography, "and now he was gone." At George M. Cohan's funeral, Dempsey "looked around and realized that we were no longer the boys we had been." And he was only

6. Whitey Ford and Phil Pepe, *Slick*, 216. Mantle and Gluck, *The Mick*, 214. Eddie Mathews and Bob Buege, *Eddie Mathews and the National Pastime*, 232. Hank Aaron and Lonnie Wheeler, *I Had a Hammer: The Hank Aaron Story*, 302.
7. Bob Gibson and Lonnie Wheeler, *Stranger to the Game*, 237.
8. Mays and Sahadi, *Say Hey*, 198.

thirty-seven at the time, an age "when most men are at their prime, [but] I was finished." Yeats may have been right when he wrote, "That is no country for old men," but only in the world of sports do men in their thirties suddenly wake up from a dream to find themselves on a cold hillside at the end of autumn.[9]

The fate of the athlete who has enjoyed a long career often resembles the literary pattern known as epic degeneration. Sagas about major epic heroes commonly exist in multiple versions that can be dated relative to one another. The primary evidence is obvious: tales of the young warrior were written first; tales that focus on the older warrior came later. By a similar logic, versions of the Arthurian legend, for example, that include Guinevere's adultery with Sir Lancelot or Arthur's betrayal by the unhappy knights Sir Agravain and Sir Modred mark a later cycle of the romance because they chronicle the life of a hero who is no longer as great as he once was.

• With a Whimper, Not a Bang

The athlete's foe, however, is not another warrior; his enemy lies within. Sometimes, it is the body that is the source of betrayal. As Bill Bradley explains in *Life on the Run*, "The real pro is . . . the veteran who tests his body each year to see if he still has it, knowing that someday he won't." Bob Pettit, a Hall of Fame basketball player in the 1950s for the St. Louis Hawks, laments in his autobiography that he was forced to endure an "inglorious end" to his career: "So this is how you go out, I thought. Sitting on the bench in Baltimore, Maryland, watching the Hawks lose by six points and unable to do anything about it." He thinks of the day he announced his retirement as "the saddest day of my life." Jerry West, a star guard for the Los Angeles Lakers, also felt like a helpless "stranger" sitting on the bench, unsympathetically stigmatized by fans and writers as being injury prone. In *Mr. Clutch* he confesses, "It's gotten so that people are afraid I'll trip over my crutches or get hurt just sitting on the bench, by falling off, and it's not funny. . . . now I can see they feel they can't

9. Dempsey and Piattelli Dempsey, *Dempsey,* 269, 255, 234. William Butler Yeats, *Selected Poems and Two Plays of William Butler Yeats,* 95. The line is from "Sailing to Byzantium."

count on me to even make it to the court." This, too, is the fate of warriors. As West's frequent opponent Bill Russell points out in *Second Wind*, there are no final victories in sports except to walk away intact.[10]

Sometimes, what fails is not the body but the spirit. The daimonic energy burns so fiercely that it often extinguishes itself before the body fails. To use Bradley's phrase, "the mind harden[s],"[11] walling itself off from the magic of the child, who turns out not to be eternal after all. In the workplace, the phenomenon is called "burnout," but the usual connotations of that term are not sufficient to explain the loss the athlete experiences. Because of the heightened drama of sports, its intensity, the "life in extremis" each contest reenacts, what "dies" is more properly thought of as a deep passion. It inevitably dies, necessarily dies, and with it so does a crucial part of the person. Hank Aaron writes about the effect of having no more records to break, and Diana Nyad was faced with the realization that "the love affair [with marathon swimming] was fading."[12] After coaching the Chicago Bears to a victory in Super Bowl XX, Mike Ditka cited the title of a Peggy Lee song, "Is That All There Is?" to express the anticlimax his career had led him to. Bill Russell was forced to admit that at the end of his playing days he could no longer do his part to make what he calls the spells of magic happen. They occurred with less and less frequency, and, worse, he says he began to "mock" the game. He lacked the daimonic spirit necessary to play "inspired" basketball, to pay proper homage to the "precious and mysterious" thing that made the game magic.[13]

The athlete also thinks of the end of his or her career as a death because it entails in many cases a loss of identity. The athlete often extends the extreme concentration required for championship-caliber play into an approach to life as well, creating a tunnel vision that denies him or her a very full existence outside of sports. Tracy Austin, who was once one of the fourteen-year-old tennis "pheenoms," confesses in *Beyond Center Court* that she had "a tennis identity only. As in: Tracy Austin equals tennis." When a serious injury ended her career,

10. Bradley, *Life on the Run*, 133. Bob Pettit and Bob Wolff, *Bob Pettit: The Drive within Me*, 3, 165. West and Libby, *Mr. Clutch*, 226. According to a January 31, 2004, article in the *Houston Chronicle*, 65 percent of NFL players leave the game with permanent injuries. Richard Justice, "Life after Football: Hello, Real World," 1B.

11. Bradley, *Life on the Run*, 221.

12. Nyad, *Other Shores*, 131.

13. Russell and Branch, *Second Wind*, 168, 167.

her identity also "disappeared." "I didn't have anything else," she realized. "I felt naked. . . . There was a huge void." Her explanation later becomes more graphic: "It was almost as if I had died on the court."[14]

Steve Garvey was a star first baseman for the Los Angeles Dodgers who cultivated the image of "the All-American boy," much to the dislike of some of his teammates, who saw it as a plastic facade. In his autobiography, however, Garvey protests his sincerity and presents himself as someone whose identity was modeled after that of two other first basemen—Lou Gehrig and his own father. When the Dodgers traded him near the end of his career to the San Diego Padres, it prefigured his "death." His assumption about being a Dodger was "I thought that would go on forever. I wanted it to." But when his boyhood dream of wearing Dodger blue ended, the feeling, he explains, "is loss, in its most profound sense, like losing yourself."[15] The following years proved Garvey right in ways he hardly expected. The image of his perfect marriage to his model-beautiful wife, Cyndy, was destroyed by the revelations of their mutual infidelities, and his long-held plans to run for political office on a conservative Republican ticket ended when he had to admit that he had fathered an illegitimate child. Even for someone like Steve Garvey who had prepared so intently for life after baseball, the end of his sports career seemed to take with it his sense of who he really was. The problem is that the athlete's identity is anchored in his body and its ability to perform.

When football player Bob Chandler sensed the "eerie feeling that this was the beginning of the end," it is significant that his description in *Violent Sundays* is, "Deep down, I knew that I really wasn't the same anymore."[16] The sensation registered first "Deep down" in the body and then passed into his consciousness. The most telling admission, however, is that *he*, not his body, wasn't the same anymore. And this discovery came to someone who had earned a law degree and would have seemed to be creating a new identity rather than losing a significant part of who he was.

Similarly, in *A False Spring* Pat Jordan expresses his loss as an inability to throw "like my old self."[17] This expression is common in

14. Austin and Brennan, *Beyond Center Court*, 128, 141.
15. Steve Garvey and Skip Rozin, *Garvey*, 180.
16. Chandler and Fox, *Violent Sundays*, 165, 167.
17. Jordan, *A False Spring*, 8.

sports, and it is not merely the literary device of synecdoche, a metaphor in which a part stands for the whole. In the athlete's situation, the body does not stand for the whole, it *is* the whole—the identity, the self. Athletes compose a large part of the gallery of American heroes, and retirement strips them of that status. Former Notre Dame football captain Michael Oriard points out that when former athletes come into the locker room to see their old teammates, they may still be celebrities but they are no longer heroes. Only those who still play the game can be heroes. In *Raging Bull* Jake La Motta confesses something similar when he recalls his loss to Irish Bob Murphy: "I had lost that self-image of indestructibility. I guess I was beginning to turn into an ordinary human, and to see myself this way frightened me."[18] The transformation of the immortal who sported on the echoing green into a mortal living under the shades of autumn traces the outlines of the pattern of decline we conceive of as epic degeneration.

Because the greater the image of indestructibility, the deeper the descent into mere mortality, the saddest portrait of the fate of warriors is found in Babe Ruth's autobiography. The last forty pages cover the transition of his life from myth to tragedy, ending with the unthinkable time when, as he refers to it earlier in the book, "baseball had no place for me." As a public performer, an athlete is dependent upon others for important aspects of his or her identity, and in the eyes of the public and the baseball establishment the real Babe Ruth disappeared at the end of his career. A 1934 trip to Paris was a "letdown," Ruth reveals, because no one recognized him. Then the Yankees gave him his unconditional release—a baseball euphemism for no longer needing someone and firing him—and no other American League team tried to sign him. Ruth was later to die of cancer, but his symbolic death began when the Yankees let him go. This unexpected turn "made me a little sick," he writes in the autobiography.[19]

The autobiography's construction of his "death" continues when he singles out a cartoon in the *New York Journal-American* that marked his passing from the scene with a picture of snapping dogs, identified as the "Ungrateful Owners" and the "Jeering Fans," chasing him

18. La Motta, Carter, and Savage, *Raging Bull,* 210.
19. Ruth and Considine, *The Babe Ruth Story,* 101, 209.

down the road "To Oblivion," as the caption read. Although he eventually signed with the Boston Braves, each day he died a little more. "I kept feeling, every time I came to bat," he remembers, "that this might be the last one." Then, like a dying man who inexplicably revives for a moment just before he finally expires, Ruth experienced one last moment of who he was. At the age of forty-one and in his twenty-second season in the majors, he hit three home runs in a game for only the fourth time in his glorious career, and one of them was the only ball ever hit over the right-field roof at Forbes Field in Pittsburgh. The momentary return of the magic restored his true identity: "for one day in Pittsburgh I again was the old Babe Ruth. For one brief day I again wore the crown of the Sultan of Swat."[20]

The rest of the autobiography describes a kind of posthumous existence. He was unceremoniously fired by the Braves before he could resign and rejected by the Yankees when they had an opening for a manager. He did return to Yankee Stadium, but only as part of a carnival-like show with Walter Johnson, the former Washington Senators pitcher. Despite the presence of sixty thousand fans, the event mattered little to Ruth because Walter Johnson "was no longer a part of the game, and the same was true of me." "It's hard," he adds, "to be on the outside of something you love. Just looking in doesn't help."[21]

In many epics, the great adventure ends with the old warrior summoning up his strength to blow a final blast of triumph from his horn. This kind of scene was not to be Babe Ruth's final act on the stage. The Yankees rejected even his appeal to manage a minor-league team, and cancer drained his once-powerful body so that on those days when he was able to get around the golf course his former drives of three hundred yards faded to weak efforts that reached only half that distance. In his autobiography he writes that all that was left was to "get [his] house in order" as a Catholic, and he sums up the end of autumn with the simple declaration, "It was a bum feeling." An outsider painfully far-removed from the joys of the echoing green, he writes what amounts to his epitaph: baseball had "forsaken the biggest drawing card it ever had."[22]

20. Ibid., 211, 212.
21. Ibid., 221.
22. Ibid., 233, 239, 221.

- **"What to Make of a Diminished Thing"**

This version of the end of autumn is not the most common one, however. Most athletes never get to complete the full arc of a career and
end up as "senior citizens." Their playing days are cut short before
they reach the stage of epic degeneration. On the other hand, their situation is not like that of the runner in A. E. Housman's famous poem,
"To an Athlete Dying Young." Because their "death" is metaphorical
rather than literal, the end of autumn becomes for them a particularly painful burden. As they construct their interpretation of the
final stage of their careers, theirs is a fate worse than living with the
sense of impermanence and fragility that shadows their playing
days. It is even worse than the epic degeneration that aging warriors
like Ruth had to face.

Roger Kahn has described the unique fate of athletes as "the
tragedy of fulfillment." The phrase captures the special agony athletes experience, but their autobiographical descriptions of their subjective response to their predicament is somewhat different from
Kahn's thesis. Kahn sees the situation, as I do when I use the phrase
"the fate of warriors," in terms of fate. But Kahn defines the tragedy
of fulfillment as the cynicism and disillusion common to the athlete
who makes the major leagues only to discover that "life remains dis-
tressingly short of ideal."[23] I find, however, that great athletes' accounts of their lives are inscribed with a different view of their fate.
What troubles them is not so much the contrast between what might
have been and what is. Rather, they must live with the painful awareness of the gulf between what was and what is. To use the title of Hakeem Olajuwon's autobiography, the great athlete has succeeded in
"living the dream," but when he is "cut," forced to quit because of injuries, or retires, the dream ends and he feels that nothing that lies
ahead is likely to come close to it.

The problem may include the loss of income. In autobiographies
written by athletes from an earlier era, that was a major considera-
tion. In the 1950s when the great Johnny Unitas played quarterback
for the Colts, who were located in Baltimore before a later owner
moved them to Indianapolis, salaries were modest and off-the-field

23. Roger Kahn, "Intellectuals and Ballplayers," 346.

earnings were a pittance, even for stars. In Unitas's autobiography *Pro Quarterback* his wife writes the "Afterword," and her main theme is that they do not live extravagantly because they know they will soon have to adjust their lifestyle to an entirely different income. And the disquieting sight of the former boxing champ panhandling on the streets or, a bit better, shaking hands with the high rollers as a Las Vegas casino greeter is a vivid reminder of the fall of the once mighty.

These stories are far less frequent today, however, because of the astronomical rise in player salaries and endorsements and the coming of the sports agent and the financial adviser. It is hard to realize that before the 1970s most players negotiated their own salaries. In fact, in *Instant Replay* former Green Bay Packer Jerry Kramer recounts the incident when all-pro center Jim Ringo dared to bring an agent with him to help negotiate his salary, and the next day coach Vince Lombardi traded him to Philadelphia. Those kinds of intimidations and threats helped swing the pendulum toward the economic realities of current sports, and as a result the modern player can normally avoid the fate of the old, washed-up fighter. Nevertheless, according to a 2004 article in the *Houston Chronicle*, 78 percent of National Football League players are unemployed, bankrupt, or divorced within two years after playing their last game.[24] The American system of capitalism encourages us to measure self-worth in terms of money, and the former athlete must often adjust his ego as well as his lifestyle.

The end of autumn also brings the loss of the spotlight. The adulation of the fans may have been an annoyance when it was a daily occurrence, but when it disappears it creates another threat to the ego. Celebrities are in part creations of the public, and diminished attention often means a diminished self. Even more troubling is the situation when the athlete finds himself confronted with the greeting, "didn't you used to be . . . ?" The passerby unintentionally reminds him that he is no longer who he was.

Underlying these issues is a deeper and more profound reality. It is what Michael Oriard, alluding to one of John Updike's novels, calls "the *Rabbit, Run* syndrome."[25] Imagine the star athlete who found the

24. Justice, "Life after Football," 1B.
25. Oriard, *The End of Autumn*, 52.

most important moments in his life under the Friday night lights at his high school football games. When that is the case, the rest of life is often a story of painful loss and decline. To have reached the top of the mountain at age eighteen creates an existence that stretches forward but without any meaningful prospects. In the case of the extraordinary athlete who finds a career in professional sports, the stakes, if not the prospects, are often raised much higher. The situation he must confront is best captured by Robert Frost in a line from his poem, "The Oven Bird": "what to make of a diminished thing."[26]

• **"Legends of the Fall"**

If the athlete's subjective experience of sports is so powerful that it allows us to conceptualize it as a kind of Eden, an echoing green, then it must follow that life after sports becomes a symbolic "fall." The "end of autumn" images in temporal form what the myth of the fall pictures spatially—an existence located outside the gates of Eden, which have closed forever. The echoing green resounded with joy, but, equally important, like all images of paradise it was a vista of limitless expansion. The end of autumn, however, is replete not just with growing darkness but also with gradual temporal and spatial restriction. It brings "closure" in a tangible sense. The athlete's dilemma is that, on the one hand, as the poet Wordsworth once wrote, "nothing can bring back the hour / Of splendour in the grass," but the future promises nothing quite so fine.[27] The end of autumn, then, is not just a crucial moment in an athlete's life when his playing career ends, but a state of mind.

The athlete must first face the loss of youth. In *A False Spring* Pat Jordan reflects upon the "fall" that takes place in the lives of all the talented players who are sniffed out by the "bird dogs," the scouts, and leave home to become professionals. When they return home, however, it is no longer the same place they left. Jordan argues that it could not be because

26. Robert Frost, *The Poetry of Robert Frost*, 120.
27. Wordsworth, *The Poetical Works of Wordsworth*, 353–54. The line is from "Ode: Intimations of Immortality from Recollections of Early Childhood."

. . . what they'd lost was the first, the purest and the most precious dream they would ever have. They'd lost perpetual youth, innocence, the dream of playing a little boy's game for the rest of their lives. In their minds, no dream would ever equal that, and so no future loss would ever affect them in the way that first one had.[28]

We were all young once and we all have dreams, but the athlete's situation is unique in certain ways and thus his dilemma is sharper and more pressing than ours. For most of us the spell of childhood magic does not last into our adult years, making us believe that we can be a Peter Pan, and most of us do not have our peak experiences at eighteen or rely on our bodies for those special moments. We can realistically see our thirties as a time of continuing to build and create, not as an irreparable "fall." Instead of contemplating with Robert Frost "what to make of a diminished thing," we can join another poet, Robert Browning, in celebrating that "the best is yet to be."[29] But that is not the way the athlete sees his experience.

In *Life on the Run* Bill Bradley tries to express his feelings about the winding down of his days as a New York Knick by quoting the novelist Joseph Conrad:

> I remember my youth and the feeling that will never come back any more—the feeling I could last forever, outlast the sea, the earth and all men; the deceitful feeling that lures us on to joys, to perils, to love, to vain effort—to death; the triumphant conviction of strength, the heat of life in the handful of dust, the glow in the heart that with every year grows dim, grows cold, grows small and expires—and expires, too soon, too soon—before life itself.[30]

For athletes the issue is more than merely mourning the passing of youth because they escaped the stumbling awkwardness that marked the adolescence of most other people. Even in those autobiographies that begin with stories of "ninety-pound weaklings" or "ugly ducklings," the master narrative the athlete traces dramatizes

28. Jordan, *A False Spring*, 136.

29. Robert Browning, *Robert Browning: Selected Poetry*, 114. The line is from "Rabbi Ben Ezra."

30. Bradley, *Life on the Run*, 126. See Joseph Conrad, *Youth and Two Other Stories*, 36–37.

the way sports metamorphosed him into a hero, someone secure in the knowledge that there was one thing he could always do with grace and skill and confidence. Lovers, dreamers, and poets may also be blessed with the ability to conjure up the daimonic to a greater degree than most other people, but because the athlete is the one who most expresses the vision in his imagination through his body, the physical contraction and fading of this "fire" bring more painful intimations.

Conrad's final thought cuts to the essence of the dilemma, what makes it a tragedy: youth dies "before life itself." The fate of the athlete is similar to that of Tithonus. Tithonus was a Trojan prince who fell in love with Aurora, the goddess of the dawn. Aurora was able to obtain for this mortal the gift of immortal life, but she failed to ask for eternal youth for him. As a result, while Aurora renews herself in beauty each morning, Tithonus must endure time's withering force, his cold, wrinkled face incapable of animation from the glowing warmth of her love and beauty. The outcome of his pact with her is that he has become, in the words of Tennyson's poetic treatment of the Greek myth, "this gray shadow, once a man— / So glorious in his beauty and thy [Aurora's] choice." This is the ultimate meaning of the end of autumn. Metaphorically, the athlete reenacts the life of Tithonus, cursed to endure immortal life without the grace of immortal youth. This is why Bradley speaks of the athlete as someone who must accept "the other side of the Faustian bargain: To live all one's days never able to recapture the feeling of those few years of intensified youth."[31] It is the "other side" of a pact with the devil in the same way that the echoing green is inextricably bound to its counter world, the end of autumn. The very qualities that make the life of a great athlete privileged are simultaneously the means of his self-destruction—one more example of why sports is a Janus world.

In his autobiography Michael Oriard relates a story that vividly illustrates this version of tragedy. His teammate on the Kansas City Chiefs, Jim Tyrer, had been an All-American at Ohio State and then became one of the dominant offensive tackles in the National Football League. He played for fourteen years and was selected for the Pro Bowl nine times. Measured by the highest standards of performance

31. Alfred Tennyson, *Selected Poetry of Tennyson*, 90. Bradley, *Life on the Run*, 190.

and the test of longevity, Tyrer was truly a great player. The quality of his play had slipped, however, by the age of thirty-five, and Hank Stram, the Chiefs' coach, traded him to the Washington Redskins. Oriard last saw Tyrer in person only moments after he had received news of the trade, and he watched him as he cleared out his locker "as if he were just another rookie who had failed to make the team."[32] When he later saw Tyrer on a Monday night telecast of a Redskins game, he was no longer a star, or even a starter, only a reserve standing on the sidelines waiting to trot on the field on fourth down with the punting team. Six years later came the shocking headline, "Ex-Chief Tackle Tyrer Kills Wife, Self." According to a police reconstruction of the crime, he had taken a .38-caliber revolver and fired a first shot that missed his wife, his childhood sweetheart with whom he lived a seemingly storybook marriage, as she lay sleeping. Then, as she awoke, screamed, and started to get out of bed, he shot her in the head and then placed the gun in his mouth and fired. The murder-suicide orphaned the four children he adored, including his son Bradley, who was the same age—seventeen—as Tyrer had been when his own father had died of a heart attack suffered while watching him play in a basketball game. Bradley was left to discover the bodies after hearing his mother's screams and the following gunshots.

According to Oriard, Tyrer was hardly the kind of person one would expect to commit such an unthinkable act. His life was far different from that of athletes whose crimes taint today's sports pages. Tyrer was not a violent man, at least not off the field, nor was he a drinker, and he played before the drug epidemic hit professional sports. He was a devoted family man, solid not just in body but in character. Oriard also stresses that the outward events of his life "read like a Frank Merriwell story."[33] Tyrer's life had been a mirror of what was best about America. He grew up in Newark, Ohio, and embodied all the virtues of small-town America and of America's "heartland." As the people of his hometown remembered him, he was not only a "coach's dream" but a fine student and a gentleman. And when a drunk driver had hit the team bus when they were returning from an away game and pushed it over an embankment, Tyrer had managed to get the emergency door open and help

32. Oriard, *The End of Autumn*, 272.
33. Ibid., 276.

his teammates and coaches escape the wreckage. Jim Tyrer was a hero.

In the six years since Tyrer's football career ended, Oriard had heard rumors about his financial difficulties. Another former teammate told him that Tyrer's business had bankrupted and that he had sold his lavish home for a more modest one. But Oriard argues that these rumors are inadequate to explain what happened. Tyrer's manner was a controlled one. He was the proverbial "meek as a kitten" off the field. Even if business problems had depressed him, they did not explain why he would also kill his wife and leave his children abandoned. Oriard says that one can speculate about the reasons for Tyrer's actions, but because of what his friends and teammates knew about him, such speculations fail to decipher the mystery of Tyrer's life.

Less of a mystery, however, is the pattern Oriard sees. He was told that the day before the killings Tyrer had taken one of his sons with him to see the Chiefs game and that after the game he had wandered around the concourse looking down on the empty stadium that had once been the center of his life. It is that image that haunts Oriard and helps to place Tyrer's act in a meaningful context. Oriard can imagine that the playing field, the echoing green of Tyrer's life, had once again mirrored to him a vision of excellence, a vision of excellence that he still demanded of himself but could no longer attain in the diminished circumstances of his life. Unlike the sixty-three-year-old Joe Williams looking at the photograph of himself in his TCU football uniform in the locker room before the Cotton Bowl of forty-two winters past, Tyrer could not say, "that guy in the picture, *that's* me." Instead, he must have seen himself as a strange doppelganger, a shadow self of the person who once was. That is what makes his death a tragedy rather than merely a senseless act of self-destruction. Oriard argues that his death was not misfortune, not simply an uncontrollable turn of the wheel of fortune, but the product of a good man's tragic flaw. Oriard concludes that the tragedy of Jim Tyrer was that "he struggled with the loss of his greatness and could not accept himself as a lesser man." And this particular flaw is more common in the world of sports than in the rest of society; the suicide rate for active and retired NFL players is six times greater than the national average.[34]

34. Ibid., 286. Justice, "Life after Football," 1B.

Both Oriard and Bradley quote in their autobiographies F. Scott Fitzgerald's statement, "there were no second acts in American lives."[35] Fitzgerald understood the centrality of youth and innocence in the American myth, and certainly the sports culture encourages athletes to live their lives as if there were no second acts. But, of course, there are. The implications of the story of Tithonus are again instructive. Just as Tithonus's fate is to live forever but without eternal youth, the fate of the athlete is that *he* "dies" but *his life* goes on. We have already seen in an earlier chapter that the athlete is sometimes like one of Peter Pan's "Lost Boys," someone who has been conditioned to live a pampered, sheltered existence that makes him dependent and unprepared for the larger social world. From another perspective, there is a simplicity and clarity to sports that does not translate to the complexities of life East of Eden. In our secular world, we "fall" not because of original sin but because innocence is necessarily shattered by the inner divisions and conflicts that are endemic to adulthood. This is especially true in the first stage of that passage, when we are primarily conscious of the anxiety produced by the experience of being sundered from the childhood feeling of wholeness and as yet unaware and unappreciative that the "fall" may become a *felix culpa,* a "fortunate fall," in the sense that it may lead to the freedom to create a more complete identity that includes a fuller consciousness of the world.[36] Many athletes, however, never move beyond the initial condition whose symptoms are feelings of diminishment and disorientation.

Jake La Motta's realization that his boxing career was over left him as dazed as he was from his opponent's blows in his final fight. "You know, it's easy enough to say," he comments about his realization that the end has come, "but what does it mean? Here I was an uneducated kid and the better part of a million bucks had gone through my hands and I was only a little better than thirty years old, and now what? What was I going to do? Where was I going?" His friend Rocky Graziano was equally lost when he could not fight anymore. "What

35. F. Scott Fitzgerald, *The Crack-Up,* 31. The line is from Fitzgerald's essay "My Lost City."

36. For a discussion of the way in which post-Enlightenment authors write psycho-autobiographies that present secularized versions of traditional biblical patterns and images, see M. H. Abrams, *Natural Supernaturalism: Tradition and Revolution in Romantic Literature.*

does Rocky Bob do when he don't fight?" he asked himself. "Learn a trade? Go on relief? Go back to robbing candy stores and Chinese laundries?"[37]

Pat Jordan's new bride had joined him for his last season in the minor leagues, and he alludes to Herman Melville's novel *Moby Dick* when he compares her to a female Ishmael who "stepped—smiling, trusting and innocent—on board a sinking ship with its mad captain." He recounts that in the shock of forgetting how to pitch, he took the mound drunk for the last game of his career, and then he and his wife packed their bags in the middle of the night and left the team before the season was over. Hall of Fame pitcher Bob Gibson also left the Cardinals ten days before the end of the 1975 season, with "no idea what I would be doing with the rest of my life," he writes in *Stranger to the Game.* In all these instances the athletes are dazed and confused because the picture they created in their minds is not complete. The pattern lacks a piece to make it clear. We have seen that this situation occurs because the end of autumn brings the athlete the sense of a premature and unnatural break in the natural alignment of the seasons.[38]

But their disorientation also reflects their response to a new reality that will trouble them as their lives move on: the unsettling lack of rhythm in the adult experiences of life. Athletes learn to perform by doing their "reps"—their repetitions. Successful performance depends upon correct execution and muscle "memory." For all of the glamour of big-time sports, the basic unit of an athlete's life is countless and endless repetitions of the same body movements. This core activity is in turn reinforced and extended into the athlete's larger world by similar behavioral structures. His or her life moves to the beat of a metronome. Practice, personal training, pregame meals, games—they all create an ordered existence that becomes as regular and natural as the seasons. Their rhythm is the physical counterpart to the ritual found in the contest itself. There is a seamless mix in sports that makes the superstition of putting on the uniform in the exact same order every day or wearing the same socks as long as the team is winning indistinguishable from the practice of going on

---

37. La Motta, Carter, and Savage, *Raging Bull,* 212–13. Rocky Graziano and Rowland Barber, *Somebody Up There Likes Me: The Story of My Life until Today,* 6.
38. Jordan, *A False Spring,* 249. Gibson and Wheeler, *Stranger to the Game,* 249.

"automatic pilot" that the baseball player uses to hit after spending countless hours in the batting cages. The athlete experiences a crucial dynamic between committing himself to this rhythm in all its manifestations and the ability to "think through the body."

Obviously, the effects of rhythm, repetition, and structure pass from the purely physical realm into the psychological. Just as the infant relies upon a set routine for its sense of well-being and growth, the athlete living on the echoing green finds the confidence and power he needs in its manifold routines and rituals. Former athletes commonly complain about the loss of the "security blanket" that sports provided for them. What made sports a sanctuary, however, was not just the authoritarian attitude of the coaches that kept them dependent children but the comforting structure that later life so frustratingly resists.

• Posthumous Existence

This mind-set makes it easy to understand why the athlete tries to delay the end of autumn. The expression in sports is "hang on," and it suggests dangling from a cliff or by a rope. It implies a life-threatening situation, one in which we hang on "for dear life." In *A False Spring* Pat Jordan explains that former athletes who become scouts and beat the bushes looking for prospects do so because the worst of all fates is to be out of the game. If we think about the nature of a cult, it is crucial for members to preserve the distinctions that separate their sanctuary from the rest of the world. Former athletes are like Mafia "wise guys," motivated not so much by money as by the desire to avoid joining the nine-to-five routine or what Jordan calls the "lunch bucket brigade." This also helps explain the fighter who goes too many rounds. Eddie Mathews, the Braves Hall of Fame third baseman, concurs that "Most of the ballplayers that continue on too long don't do it because of the money. They just don't want to give up the ghost. They want to go back and be 25 years old again."[39]

Mathews's image of the ghost is a recurring motif in other autobiographies. In some instances the dreams of the young player are re-

39. Mathews and Buege, *Eddie Mathews and the National Pastime*, 239.

placed by the dreams of the older player, but because the older player has reached the end of autumn and has experienced a kind of death, these latter daydreams represent a kind of postmortem consciousness. Bob Gibson confesses in *Stranger to the Game,* "Strange as it sounds, twice a week or so I still dream that I'm playing the game. In the dreams it's always before a game . . . and I'm supposed to pitch. . . . But I never get around to actually throwing the ball."[40] It is almost as if Gibson is a ghost haunting the house where he once lived and unable to do what he once did so magnificently—pitch.

The nightmare Mickey Mantle relates in his autobiography is an even more graphic example of postmortem consciousness:

> I had a recurring nightmare: coming to Yankee Stadium in a cab, wearing my uniform. Trying to crawl through a hole. I can see Whitey and Billy and Casey and my other teammates. I'm supposed to be with them, but I can't squeeze through the hole in the wall. I'm stuck. I hear the public address speaker blare out my name. "At bat . . . number seven . . . Mickey Mantle. . . ." That's when I wake up, drenched in sweat. . . . recently I've been having another bad dream. I have died and I'm buried. But somehow I'm floating above my grave, reading the words on my tombstone: HERE LIES MICKEY CHARLES MANTLE. BANNED FROM BASEBALL.[41]

Double consciousness, a trope famously discussed by W. E. B. DuBois in *The Souls of Black Folk,* is a distinctive theme in autobiographies by African Americans, but it also appears fairly often in sports autobiographies written by white athletes as well as black athletes. Dreams and nightmares like those of Gibson and Mantle reflect that psychic division, but in them we find, more specifically, the person mourning the death of the athlete he once was. The ghosts that rise in the dreams know that they belong on the field with their teammates or that it is their turn to pitch for the team, but because they are dead, that cannot happen. These are the shades that haunt the end of autumn.

Ball Four begins with the dream of the thirty-year-old Jim Bouton, who is "dying" as an athlete:

40. Gibson and Wheeler, *Stranger to the Game,* 274.
41. Mantle and Gluck, *The Mick,* 235–36.

I dream my knuckleball is jumping around like a Ping-Pong ball in the wind and I pitch a two-hit shutout against my old team, the New York Yankees, single home the winning run in the ninth inning and, when the game is over, take a big bow on the mound in Yankee Stadium with 60,000 people cheering wildly. After the game reporters crowd around my locker asking me to explain exactly how I did it. I don't mind telling them.

I dream I have pitched four consecutive shutouts for the Seattle Pilots and the Detroit Tigers decide to buy me in August for their stretch drive. It's a natural: the Tigers give away a couple of minor-league pheenoms, and the Pilots, looking to the future, discard an aging right-handed knuckleballer. I go over to Detroit and help them win the pennant with five saves and a couple of spot starts. I see myself in the back of a shiny new convertible riding down Woodward Avenue with tickertape and confetti covering me like snow. I see myself waving to the crowd and I can see people waving back, smiling, shouting my name.

I dream my picture is on the cover of *Sports Illustrated* in October and they do a special "Comeback of the Year" feature on me, and all winter long I'm going to dinners and accepting trophies as the Comeback Player of the Year.[42]

Unlike the dreams of Gibson and Mantle, Bouton's dreams are in part fantasies. But they have some implications similar to those of the other two players. Bouton claims that he actually had these dreams; they are not daydreams or carefully constructed fictions. It is his age, however, that gives them a context that adds to their meaning. Bouton was once a twenty-game-winning fastball pitcher, but now the arm that could throw with such velocity is, in the parlance of the game, "dead." He has now been reduced to throwing the knuckleball, "holding on—literally—with his fingertips," he says, punning on the distinctive grip used to throw that pitch. Unlike the powerful fastball, the knuckleball is considered a "junk" pitch, appropriate for the "aging veteran"—he's thirty!—who is on the verge of being discarded himself.

In this case, the postmortem consciousness is that of his arm displaced into his mind by a kind of ventriloquism. He confesses he sometimes hears a voice that whispers to him that he can find his old fastball and once again be the great pitcher he used to be. He calls the

42. Bouton and Shecter, *Ball Four*, xv-xvi.

voice a "siren song." He in turn "whisper[s] lovingly" to his arm, "Things could be like that again. Just one more time, one more season." In his tragi-comic vision, the myth of Tithonus has a bizarre twist: he looks and feels as if he were in his early twenties, but he adds, "My arm, however, is over a hundred years old." As diminished as the power of his arm is, all it takes is speculation that he might be traded to the Washington Senators to revive his willingness to make the Faustian bargain: "I still think I have a chance to be a hero someplace." Even after he retired from baseball and spent almost nine years as an actor and a sportscaster for the ABC flagship station in New York City, he tried to make a comeback at age thirty-nine and was briefly called up from the minors by the Atlanta Braves. As he wrote earlier in *Ball Four*, "The sirens are still singing."[43]

The version of postmortem consciousness that we find in some sports autobiographies is one form of the construction of death that the athlete must undertake when he or she reaches the end of autumn. We can also view the "farewell tours" around the league that some great athletes make as another construction of death. The athlete is usually honored with tributes and gifts and the fans have a last opportunity to express their admiration, but the tone of the ritual is funereal. The person being honored is rarely the athlete who takes the court or field that night, but the great athlete who once was. Willie Mays, for example, had been urged to retire after the 1967 season, but he refused until after the 1973 season. By that time, he had been traded from the San Francisco Giants to the New York Mets, and as a member of this team Mays had to concede, "I really felt like a spare part."[44] The metaphor is a cliché, but a telling cliché. Instead of his former sense of wholeness and of a life animated by the spirit, Mays now describes a diminished, mechanical existence.

For boxers, there is another ritual that serves as a kind of construction of death. At championship fights, it is customary for former greats to attend and be recognized by the ring announcer or the commissioner before the bout begins. As Joe Louis watched the 1951 Jersey Joe Walcott–Ezzard Charles championship fight, he felt eerily displaced from himself. "I almost felt dead," he writes in his autobiography, "like

43. Ibid., 19, 55, 36, 297, 49.
44. Mays and Sahadi, *Say Hey*, 273.

some kind of ghost looking on."[45] Later, when he was reduced to
wrestling to support himself, his wife told him that it was like seeing
President Eisenhower wash the dishes. And the bell tolled, but in a different way, for Jack Dempsey when the commissioner forgot to intro-
duce him before the Muhammad Ali–Joe Frazier fight. Dempsey says
in his autobiography that previous celebrations of him had both
moved and saddened him because he knew that occasions of public acclaim were dwindling for him.

In a way, these constructions of death hearken back to Oriard's distinction that the former athlete cannot be a hero, only a celebrity. There
is a certain kind of acclaim that has the tone of a eulogy. It bespeaks
reverence for the dead rather than joy in the living. Carl Yastrzemski,
the Hall of Fame left fielder for the Boston Red Sox, experienced a
metamorphosis from living hero to marble icon. "Something strange
was going on," he writes about the fans' view of him when he reached
his late thirties. "I was becoming an object of curiosity and affection."
The implications became clearer when he approached forty. His perception is that he was the "elder statesman," "a fixture in Boston,"
and "a must-see on an itinerary of New England." He had become
not just a historical monument but his own headstone. And the death
mask had been appropriately fitted for the sarcophagus, for when the
Red Sox were eliminated from the pennant race in his final season, the
man who once was so intense that he used to think about jumping off
the Mystic River Bridge after a bad game was gone. "When I made an
out it didn't eat me up inside anymore," he realized. "What was
wrong with me? I didn't want to kill myself after making an out. I
didn't feel like crap when we lost."[46]

- **"Free at Last!"**

While Tithonus and Updike's fictional Rabbit Angstrom epitomize
the fate of many athletes, not all athletes approach the end of autumn
with a sense of self-diminishment and decline. Another significant
response, though not so common, is a feeling of relief and release.

45. Joe Louis and Edna and Art Rust, Jr., *Joe Louis: My Life*, 214.
46. Yastrzemski and Eskenazi, *Yaz*, 267, 289, 294.

The dramatic intensity of sports performance has as its counterpart an equally deep pressure. The pressure derives in part from the impermanence and fragility of the way of life, never knowing when a sudden injury or a talented rookie will bring about the end of it all. The greatest pressure for the star athlete, however, descends upon him from the weight of his or her own standards of excellence as well as the expectations of the fans. In *Second Wind*, for example, Bill Russell describes his life as the hub of the Boston Celtics dynasty as a "compression chamber," and he confesses that when he retired he left behind all the "encumbrances"—Boston, his wife of thirteen years, children, friends, and material possessions.[47] The experience was a kind of death—the star died and he became a person, Russell says—and he felt the exciting liberation that it brought.

His former teammate Bob Cousy provides a more extended discussion of this perspective in *The Last Loud Roar*. The autobiography begins during the championship playoff series with the Los Angeles Lakers in 1963. Cousy had always been a little man in a world of giants, but he, too, felt like a freak because of his abnormally long arms and massive hands. His point of view about the end of his career is unmistakable. "I want it over," he says. He was unhappy with his play during the game. He had fouled a lot that night, a sign he was getting older and slower. On the other hand, he was glad the Celtics lost the game and the series would continue, because he was retiring and did not want to go out after a bad game. The conflicting emotions were not new. Throughout his career, he confesses, he had possessed the cockiness of a great athlete but could never escape the chronic fear "that this would be the night it would all desert me, that this would be the game where everything would go bad and I would be out there, exposed and helpless."[48]

For Cousy, the burden had only been magnified over the years because of all the championships and personal awards. For the last three years of his career he was a hermit, staying in his hotel room on road trips, reading or watching television, even having his meals sent up by room service. Even more stressful, the pressure had created a nervous eye tic, and he had nightmares in which he reverted to speaking the French language of his childhood. Some nights he had

47. Russell and Branch, *Second Wind*, 215.
48. Bob Cousy and Ed Linn, *The Last Loud Roar*, 16, 20.

to tie one of his arms to the bed because he would run in his sleep. He points out that over the last seven years the other star on the team, Bill Russell, had never gone into an important game without throwing up in the locker room before the contest.

The problem was not fear of losing or the fact that the thrill had gone. "I'm thirty-four years old," he writes, "and I'm still a boy having to prove myself over again every time out." The pressure came from the inner demand to reaffirm his identity by living up to the highest standards of performance. "I've earned the right," he tells himself, ". . . to leave as I came. To be remembered for what I was at the top of my game." It is interesting that he says he still loves the game itself, the competition. His daimonic fires still burn brightly. What he hates is nakedly exposing himself before the fans, whom he describes as a screaming mob at a carnival. Before games he now lies in bed until the last minute, dreading the moment when he has to get up and dress to go to the arena. "[T]he time comes in a man's life, dammit," he angrily vents, "where he shouldn't allow himself to be spat upon for a $2.50 ticket."[49] Obviously, the price of admission has dramatically increased since Cousy's era, but the pressure has remained unrelentingly the same. Sports is a war in a number of ways, but some warriors willingly exchange their swords for ploughshares, savoring the freedom it brings after years of living on the edge.

Ted Williams felt the same way as Cousy when the end of autumn came for him. The first sentence of his autobiography, *My Turn at Bat,* is "I'm glad it's over." Unlike other players who wanted to remain forever on the echoing green, who were desperate not to be "out of the game," Williams makes it clear from the beginning that he has no "youth wish." He set out to become the greatest hitter who ever lived, and many writers, fans, and fellow baseball players would readily agree that he succeeded. But the pressure created by this expectation was enormous. He focuses in the opening pages on "how I thought the weight of the damn world was always on my neck, grinding on me."[50] Clearly, Williams feels anger, but there is also pride that a poor kid from an unhappy home in San Diego who was not well-educated or particularly smart played probably the only game in which he could have excelled. But mostly there is relief that the pressure is off.

49. Ibid., 21, 50–51.
50. Williams and Underwood, *My Turn at Bat,* 7.

He says he has found a sustained freedom that he could experience during his career only when he was off the diamond fishing alone somewhere in Maine.

The sense of freedom sometimes has little to do with the pressure, however, and lies elsewhere. The self-aware athlete knows that he is a captive of his fame. Because he is a celebrity, his identity is often imposed upon him. Wilt Chamberlain tired of being "Wilt the Stilt," an image that he felt marginalized him as a carnival attraction without regard to his wide-ranging interests, and Bill Bradley found the media portrayal of him at Princeton as the Christian scholar-athlete to be a straitjacket. Chet Walker, who left the NBA for a career as a television producer, argues in his autobiography *Long Time Coming* that no athlete can know who he is as long as he is in the game because an athlete's self-image is defined for him by others and their expectations. When he retired, his overwhelming feeling was of freedom. He could finally say, "Nobody owned me," neither the white owners with their reserve clause nor the fans with their adulation of his public persona. Ty Cobb's fiery independence led him to a similar conclusion. He had invested his money in the Detroit automobile industry and in Coca-Cola stock and became a multimillionaire who, unlike many other players, could not be treated like a dependent child by the club owners. When he retired, his attitude was "You're free, I told myself."[51]

Other players also left the game on their own terms. When Michael Oriard was suddenly cut by the Kansas City Chiefs, he played a season in the Canadian Football League so that he could end his career positively rather than with the memory of the anger, bitterness, and hurt he felt after he was dismissed by the Chiefs. He had always planned to be an English professor, and, like the good student he was, he approached football as another teacher. The lesson he learned was a very positive one: "Like a good teacher, football taught me how to leave it behind." His retirement from football was a death, but it was, for him, a "little death," and, even better, "a prelude to rebirth" as a graduate student at Stanford and later a faculty member at Oregon State. Jackie Robinson also avoided what Bradley calls "the other side of the Faustian bargain." He did not have to give the Devil his due be-

51. Walker and Messenger, *Long Time Coming*, 249. Ty Cobb and Al Stump, *My Life in Baseball: The True Record*, 259.

cause, he writes, "The way I figured it, I was even with baseball and baseball with me."[52] Robinson could retire with this kind of equanimity because, like Bradley and Oriard, he had other interests. He had accepted an executive position with Chock Full O' Nuts, and the horizon already included working with the NAACP and other political causes.

The secret, some perceptive athletes argue, is not only having other interests but seeing sports as a stage in life rather than as life itself. Jim Brown, considered by many the greatest running back in NFL history, retired suddenly at the height of his career with the Cleveland Browns. In *Out of Bounds*, he is typically blunt with his opinions: "I looked at football as a waterhole when you're crossing the desert. You stop, enjoy the scenery, sip a little water, get your ass out of there."[53] He then moved on to a career in the movies and later involvement in social causes working with inmates in California prisons and with youth gangs in Los Angeles. Bob Chandler, who left professional football for a career as a lawyer, admits in *Violent Sundays* that life after football meant losing the sheltered existence of the eternal child. "Life was so secure under that helmet," he says with some nostalgia. But he says he found a fuller humanity in opening himself up to the contingencies of an adult world. He concludes his autobiography with the traditional image of the warrior who knows his time has come, but he adds his realization that the inevitable "fall" that creates the end of autumn may ultimately lead to another important stage of development: "as with every professional athlete, the time had come to strip away the armor, leaving a vulnerability from which to grow." Wilt Chamberlain also looked positively on the end of his career in basketball. In *Wilt* he muses on the rich variety of possibilities before him and concludes his autobiography with the thought that "this book doesn't really have an ending."[54]

As we have seen, however, that is not the usual fate of warriors. The intensity of sports, the passion required for this world in which the athlete lives on the edge, means that the athlete channels into the game the daimonic energy that might have been devoted elsewhere.

52. Oriard, *The End of Autumn*, xix, 324. Robinson and Duckett, *I Never Had It Made*, 122.
53. Brown and Delsohn, *Out of Bounds*, 112.
54. Chandler and Fox, *Violent Sundays*, 180. Chamberlain and Shaw, *Wilt*, 310.

As many athletes admit in their autobiographies, what they feel for their sport is a passion in the sense of a love. Joe DiMaggio speaks for many others in the "Acknowledgments" to *Lucky to Be a Yankee:* "To Baseball, . . . which has been and always will be my first love." In his autobiography Joe Louis discusses his many extramarital affairs, including those with Lena Horne and Lana Turner, but he proudly testifies, "There was never a time I felt unfaithful to my profession, and in boxing that's saying a lot."[55]

Sports autobiographies are filled with images that reflect this view of the athlete's conception of his or her relationship with sports. From a young age these privileged people are "courted." We have already seen in the chapter "Body Songs" Bill Bradley's thoughts about the similarity between the way society views the athlete and the way it looks at beautiful girls. Furthermore, this intense love for the game is so powerful that it becomes addictive. We have seen the force of the adrenaline "rush" and the transporting effect of those "magic" moments on the court or the field. This metaphoric conception of sports is summed up in the titles used by former football players Chip Oliver and Lyle Alzado: *High for the Game* and *Mile High.* It is also common for athletes to discuss the problem created by the end of their careers as a "withdrawal" from an "addiction." The implications of the metaphors of love and drugs come together as ways of conceptualizing and understanding the daimonic. Just as the end of autumn brings to a close the joys of sporting on the echoing green, withdrawal chases away the high and love's embers fade. As Tracy Austin says, using a buried image suggestive of love, "The sport was deserting me; I wasn't deserting it."[56]

• **The Final Act**

Consider a final metaphor. When the playing days are over, the stage darkens and the athlete must exit. But the problem is that only two acts at most have been written, and there is no definite script for the acts that lie ahead. Jerry Kramer, the star guard on the great Green Bay

55. DiMaggio, *Lucky to Be a Yankee.* Louis, Rust, and Rust, Jr., *Joe Louis,* 226.
56. Austin and Brennan, *Beyond Center Court,* 136.

Packer championship teams of the 1960s, speaks for many athletes who have come to the end of autumn. In *Instant Replay*, Kramer writes, "my life's always been easy. I've never had to fight for anything. I've always been able to do almost anything I wanted to do without great effort, almost naturally." His diary later records his thoughts after the Packers' Super Bowl victory over the Oakland Raiders, as he muses about the possibility of retiring soon and admits, even with all his personal and team triumphs, "My life seems a little empty." Even more telling, however, he remains in the locker room after almost everyone else has gone, and the last sentence in the diary is, "I wanted to keep my uniform on as long as I possibly could."[57] It is very hard to go gentle into what is rarely that good night.

---

57. Kramer and Schaap, *Instant Replay*, 55, 233.

5

"Something Old,
Something New,
Something Borrowed,
Something Blue"

*Dennis Rodman and the Contemporary
Athlete as Postmodern Celebrity*

THE ATHLETES I HAVE FEATURED MOST PROMINENTLY IN
this study span a wide historical arc ranging from baseball's
first Hall of Fame selection, Ty Cobb, whose baseball career
began in the pre–World War I era, to more recent stars such as tennis
player Tracy Austin, but whatever their individual differences, in
narrating their subjective experiences of sports this broad and varied
chorus of athletes has revealed some important recurring motifs,
themes, and issues. The commonality and pervasiveness of the
points of view, patterns, and subjects have little significant variabil-
ity because of the historical era, the particular sport, or the status of
the athlete—whether he was a star like Jackie Robinson and Bill
Bradley or relatively unknown like Michael Oriard and Lynda Huey.

I have not mentioned until now what has become a major subject
in sports studies: the increasing role of the media, particularly television. Many older sports autobiographies refer to the once pervasive shibboleth inscribed as a warning in the shrine of the locker
room: "What you say here, what you do here, let it stay here, when
you leave here." There is something quaint about such a notion in a

media-saturated age of tabloid journalism and twenty-four-hour television channels devoted exclusively to sports. While "the Eye altering alters all," nothing has altered sports more than the glaring eye
of the media. In writing about the "frenzy" of fame in the contemporary world, Leo Braudy emphasizes "the crucial awareness of audience that marks our time."[1] We may have once mythologized the
athlete as "The Natural," but the ideal of athletes unself-consciously
losing themselves in the "magic" of play is now only a possibility,
not a daily reality. Today performance always brings with it awareness of audience, and the athlete's consequent self-consciousness indelibly colors his or her subjective experience of sports.

No contemporary figure captures better than Dennis Rodman the
sensibility and point of view of athletes whose constructions of their
self-images are shaped by the realities of a celebrity culture.

• Dress for Success

In 1996 Dennis Rodman famously wore a wedding dress to a New
York bookstore signing to promote the publication of his autobiography, *Bad as I Wanna Be,* and MTV filmed the event for its upcoming
reality program, "Rodman World Tour." The staged media event was
symbolic in a number of respects. Most obviously, it marked the increasing role that sports plays as a branch of entertainment as opposed to its more traditional role as an imaginative construct that
mirrors national values, particularly those values informed by the
belief that sports is a democratic meritocracy and that its vision of
masculinity fosters important qualities of leadership. The manipu-
lated "frenzy" surrounding the event also reinforced that contemporary athletes are among the most prominent figures in our celebrity
culture. The origins of this trend date to the 1920s and 1930s when
movie stars and athletes began to replace statesmen and business ty-
coons as America's heroes and idols,[2] and the athlete's celebrity sta-

---

1. Blake, *Selected Poetry and Prose of Blake,* 84. The "Eye altering alters all" line
is from "The Mental Traveller." Leo Braudy, *The Frenzy of Renown: Fame and Its
History,* 587.
2. See Leo Lowenthal's chapter, "The Triumph of Mass Idols," in *Literature,
Popular Culture, and Society,* 109–40, and Rader, "Compensatory Sport Heroes."

tus has only increased with the expansion of the media to round-the-clock television sports programming and "tell it like it is" and exposé journalism.

The wedding dress was not a mere prop but a "costume" that revealed the role Rodman was playing and its cultural significance. It was an icon of the literal trappings—the outer accoutrements—that not only signify but *are* fame in a society in which fame is often separated from achievement.[3] In this case a key element of the costume's meaning was its parodic mixture of the sacred and the profane, a conflation and a contradiction central to Rodman's construction of self. While Rodman's performance on this and other occasions may seem to be all about flamboyance rather than substance, like other gestures of celebrity, it is not content-less. It may not have the intellectual qualities that we normally associate with wit, but it is witty in the literal sense of Dr. Samuel Johnson's famous eighteenth-century definition of the cardinal trait of metaphysical poetry: a *discordia concors*, a violent yoking together of opposites. The wedding dress and accessories with their "something old, something new, something borrowed, something blue," become an apt symbol for Rodman's self-image in his autobiography *Bad as I Wanna Be*, a book that presents the contemporary athlete as a postmodern celebrity, a figure composed of contradictory strands that make him an appropriate representative of the Janus world of sports.

Perhaps the physical intelligence of athletes and our subliminal recognition of the presence of what I have called the daimonic in sports performance justify the common references to sports "heroes," but historian Daniel J. Boorstin's analysis of the distinction between the hero and the celebrity makes it clear that the latter is the appropriate term for the athlete. Boorstin argues that the hero requires the "passage of time" for his "gestation," whereas the celebrity "is always a contemporary." The form of the medium is also important.

In *The Image: A Guide to Pseudo-Events in America* Daniel J. Boorstin also reviews the biographical articles in the *Saturday Evening Post* and *Collier's* and finds a similar shift between 1914 and the 1920s from articles about people in politics, business, and the professions to articles about people in the world of entertainment and from articles about people in high art to articles about people in popular culture, 59.

3. Braudy, *The Frenzy of Renown*, 587. I am also indebted to Braudy's ideas about the relationship of fame to performance and costumes.

"The hero is made by folklore, sacred texts and history books," but "the celebrity is the creature of gossip, of public opinion, of magazines, newspapers, and the ephemeral images of movie and television screen." The title of Margo Jefferson's 1997 piece on Rodman in the *New York Times* is pointed when it presents him as "Man of the Moment."[4]

- ## "Very Well Then I Contradict Myself"

Although Rodman's ultimate fate, like that of other celebrities, is to be destroyed by the passage of time rather than created and established by it, he fascinates the media because he captures the zeitgeist of a wrinkle in time if not of an age. Even *The Chronicle of Higher Education*, a highly respected academic periodical, featured in a 1996 issue a call by two scholars for their colleagues to make Rodman the subject of cultural studies research, and in the following years Rodman became perhaps second only to Michael Jordan as the subject of scholarly articles about current athletes. Those articles usually present one of two opposing theses about Rodman: either he is a subversive figure, particularly in matters of race, gender, and sexual orientation, or despite his flamboyance and cultivation of controversy, his image is ultimately a traditional one. On the one hand, his style on and off the court would place him in the line of what scholars like Todd Boyd call "bad niggas," rebellious black athletes such as boxers Jack Johnson and Muhammad Ali, as opposed to "Uncle Toms" like boxer Joe Louis, who, along with other black athletes on this side of the cultural divide, was often described as "a credit to his race." Similarly, LaFrance and Rail use the jacket cover of Rodman's later autobiography, *Walk on the Wild Side*, which depicts him as a kind of human tiger, as part of their arguments that he is a "postmodern savage," a concept that emphasizes his blackness, phallocentrism, and sexuality, and that other photographs and images in the book suggest he is a "racially coded monster," a King Kong with all the Hollywood associations found in the "resurrection of anthro-

4. Boorstin, *The Image*, 62–63. Margo Jefferson, "Dennis Rodman, Bad Boy as Man of the Moment," C13.

pomorphic ape representations in late twentieth-century America." (In *Walk on the Wild Side*, Rodman reports that he told model Cindy Crawford, "there's a monster in my pants.") Other commentators, however, take a diametrically opposite view of Rodman, interpreting such images as cartoons that depict him as a "ridiculous court jester" and "a sort of postmodern [Peter] Pan" whose persona was "borrowed from the gay nightclub scene."[5]

As perceptive as these interpretations are, their limitation is that they seize upon one aspect of Rodman's construction of self as the defining issue rather than granting Rodman credit for creating a persona characterized by contradictions. In an era in which the costume is the self and the style is the substance, Rodman appropriates and caricatures in a postmodern way the Whitmanesque celebration of the self: "Do I contradict myself? / Very well then I contradict myself, / I am large, I contain multitudes."[6] The blueprint Rodman draws for *Bad as I Wanna Be* combines traditional American autobiographical tropes with an opposing pop version of counterculture values. The result is a performance of self in which, as the then-current black vernacular implied, bad is good.

Although Boorstin argues that the celebrity "is born in the daily papers and never loses the mark of his fleeting origin," Rodman claims as a central thesis in *Bad as I Wanna Be* that he was born in his own imagination: "I made myself." He brings a more contemporary angle of vision to that process, however, than athletes writing even one or two decades earlier. Whereas Billie Jean King, for example, spoke for most other athletes when she wrote in her 1982 autobiography that she knew as a child she wanted to be "the best in one

---

5. The title of the *Chronicle* article is "Professors Call for Papers on Basketball's Dennis Rodman," A18. Todd Boyd, "The Day the Niggaz Took Over: Basketball, Commodity Culture, and Black Masculinity," 133–37. Mélisse Lafrance and Geneviève Rail, "Excursions into Otherness: Understanding Dennis Rodman and the Limits of Subversive Agency," 42, 44, 45. Also see Mélisse Lafrance and Geneviève Rail, "As Bad as He Says He Is?: Interrogating Dennis Rodman's Subversive Potential." For a discussion of the implications of the latter image, see my earlier chapter "Body Songs," 86–95. Dennis Rodman and Michael Silver, *Walk on the Wild Side*, 140. Michelle Dunbar, "Dennis Rodman—Do You Feel Feminine Yet?: Black Masculinity, Gender Transgression, and Reproductive Rebellion on MTV," 268. Steve Johnson, "Trash Talk," as quoted in Lafrance and Rail, "As Bad as He Says He Is?" 75.

6. Walt Whitman, *Leaves of Grass*, 88. The passage is from "Song of Myself."

thing," Rodman boasts that he always knew he "would be famous someday."[7] The distinction is telling. The way to fame in contemporary America does not necessarily require achievement, being the best at something, but performance. And what Rodman performs in *Bad as I Wanna Be* is a "fractured fairy tale."

• Dennis's "Fractured Fairy Tale"

What attracted Rodman's primary audience for the book—an audience that he specifically identifies as "the grunge crowd, the Generation X types"[8]—are the more flamboyant riffs of his Pearl Jam–inspired version of "Song of Myself." They love all his gestures of defiance, his colloquial and slang language, the song lyrics he quotes, and the playful use of huge fonts and boldface type. Even though these devices and gestures are important marketing tools, Rodman first places his story into the comfortable contours of the most traditional American trope: the myth of rags to riches. The plot he relates is classic Horatio Alger or Benjamin Franklin, a narrative in which virtue is tested by adversity and rewarded with financial success. The main episodes are common to the pattern: he grew up in the projects of Dallas, his father abandoned the family when Rodman was three years old, after high school he worked as a janitor on the graveyard shift at the Dallas–Fort Worth Airport, he became a petty thief, he was homeless for a while, but after miraculously growing nine inches after high school and developing the commensurate basketball skills while playing at little Southeastern Oklahoma University he became a star in the National Basketball Association.

The metaphor he chooses in *Bad as I Wanna Be* to describe his early life is taken from his experiences sneaking into the Texas State Fair. He and his friends used to work their way through a dark and scary sewage tunnel five miles to the fair, and he compares his childhood to that black hole with the only light to be found on the top side of the manhole cover they used to get into the fair. The tunnel symbolizes the extra difficulties incurred by the underclass on their journey to

---

7. Boorstin, *The Image,* 63. Rodman and Keown, *Bad as I Wanna Be,* 7. King and Deford, *Billie Jean,* 56. Rodman and Keown, *Bad as I Wanna Be,* 6.
8. Rodman and Keown, *Bad as I Wanna Be,* 69.

success as well as a twisted version of the American celebration of the road not taken. It is also a grave from which his traditional American pluck and self-reliance allow him to resurrect himself, and he says he carried the memory of this past with him to the NBA where it is responsible for his success.

Even his playing style in the NBA testifies to his respect for traditional virtues. For all his flamboyance and grunge trappings off the court, his self-image as a player is that he is a "blue-collar worker." His forte is rebounding, the nonglamorous, dirty "grunt work" that he believes causes the factory workers of Detroit to identify with him. His defensive-minded game that relies upon brute strength and physical intimidation is an on-court mirror of the "rugged individualism" of the Horatio Alger story. During the game he is not in the spotlight, he claims, but once again in a kind of tunnel: "I'm the basketball version of a gravedigger. Rebounding and playing defense is like putting bodies in the hole." This may seem like a strange latter-day version of Ben Franklin's American tradesman story, but it is clear that Rodman values its character-building power. His identity as a blue-collar worker testifies to the integrity he believes he has maintained in the midst of all his fame and fortune. In fact, the stance he takes as an iconoclastic rebel is based upon this claim of integrity. Like the controversial athletes of the 1960s, he presents himself as a purist for whom the "game is sacred, almost holy."[9] His guiding premise is that the team and the game come first, and he protests the corruption of the game by those who see it only as entertainment and business. Most knowledgeable sportswriters admired Rodman's on-court performance, and we can accept to a certain degree his characterization of himself as the ultimate "gamer" whose defiant pride is very much in the tradition of American independence and individualism.

He parallels his Franklinesque rise in sports with his version of the traditional bildungsroman theme of the protagonist's search for the father. His father, the aptly named Philander Rodman, simply stopped coming home one day and Rodman never saw him again. He grew up without a male role model, and he confesses that living in an otherwise all-female household he even developed fears that he might be gay.

9. Ibid., 108, 78, 86.

The next part of his autobiography shifts from the black urban world of Dallas to the starkly contrasting farmlands of Bokchito, Oklahoma, where he creates a strange version of the traditional American dream.

When he got a scholarship to play basketball at Southeastern Oklahoma University, he decided that he had to leave behind Dallas and everything that went with it—his mother, the rest of his family, and "a lot of myself." In Oklahoma he reinvents himself and invents a family. That summer while he was helping coach at the university's basketball camp for kids, he met Bryne Rich, a troubled thirteen-year-old who had killed his best friend in a hunting accident. The rest of the story brings an unusual twist to the usual pattern: "Bryne told his parents he wanted a little brother. He got me instead." What Rodman implies *he* got was the childhood he never had in the Dallas projects and the American dream of a nuclear family, complete with the house with the white picket fence. But of course it's not just the fence that is white, but the entire world he's about to enter. Rodman soon moved out of the dorms and went to live with the Riches in the tiny nearby town of Bokchito. For Rodman the Riches' farm was a "haven" and Mr. Rich the father he never had. He credits James Rich with bringing out the human side he had repressed, giving him the discipline and guidance he lacked, and modeling a positive approach to life. But this part of Rodman's story goes well beyond that kind of psychological analysis and becomes a revealing imaginative construction of a lost boy's journey home. When he says he came to consider the Riches his "real family," tells Bryne he'd like to be adopted as his brother, and characterizes James Rich as "like an old wise man in a fairy tale," the elements of fantasy break to the surface of the narrative, and Rodman admits this stage in his life was in many ways "an unreal scene."[10]

The twenty-two-year-old black man from the inner-city projects started getting up at 5 a.m. to milk the cows and do other farm chores. Even stranger, because he was a giant black man in an almost all-

10. Ibid., 29, 23. Rodman, Rich, and Steinberg, *Rebound*, 89. Rodman and Pat Rich alternate writing the chapters, and much of the autobiography focuses on their different perspectives on race during the period when Rodman found life on the Rich family farm a "haven" from the racial animosity he felt at college. Pat Rich was able to accept Rodman as a member of the family not only because of Bryne's affection for him but also because she believed that God had sent Rodman to take care of the family after Bryne accidentally killed his best friend. Rodman and Keown, *Bad as I Wanna Be*, 29, 28, 23.

white rural society, people assumed he was Bryne's father or Bryne's mother Pat's lover. Pat Rich was also a student at Southeastern Oklahoma, and she and Rodman carpooled every day. Not surprisingly, she had a great deal of difficulty handling the situation. In Rodman's first autobiography, *Rebound,* he and Pat Rich alternately write the chapters, and they detail episodes that are both funny and painful, such as their descriptions of Pat Rich lying down in the backseat of the family car so that the townspeople of Bokchito would not know she was in the car as Rodman drove through the dusty streets. Although the contradictions and paradoxes that puncture Rodman's fantasy of family life with the Riches shape this part of the autobiography into a bizarre new kind of "American Gothic," the implication is that it is a discovery of a kind of Eden, a sanctuary filled with the love and support that should have been his during his childhood. This "life with father" serves as the necessary premise for the traditional rise that was to follow, a rise that affirms the national myths of meritocracy and upward social mobility.

The power of the Rich family to transform the black kid from the ghetto is only the prelude to the very different metamorphosis of Rodman by the celebrity culture during his career as a professional athlete. Like the Roman god Janus, usually represented in statuary with a double-faced head, each looking in the opposite direction, the self-image Rodman constructs in *Bad as I Wanna Be* is both one thing and its opposite at the same time. He is "something old, something new"—the traditional rags-to-riches hero, and the subversive new-age athlete who challenges conventional notions of race, gender, and sexuality; he is "something borrowed, something blue"—a "throwback" athlete who sacrifices the glamour of scoring to concentrate on rebounding and defense for the good of the team, and the obscenity-spouting writer who graphically confesses the details of his affair with Madonna. His subjective experience of sports is that it is a stage where the self-made man turns into the self-styled performer.

- **"Nothing Succeeds Like Excess": Dennis as the Vulgar Dandy**

The image of the athlete as showman begins before we even begin to read the text of *Bad as I Wanna Be.* Instead of the usual headshot or photograph of the athlete in action, on the cover Rodman is nude and

mounted on a powerful Harley-Davidson motorcycle with a basketball teasingly placed to cover his genitals. The phallic dimension is
the first of several signs that he is a larger-than-life figure. The image
introduces the theme of badness and its corollary: "nothing succeeds
like excess."[11] The author of this famous twist on the traditional
proverb is Oscar Wilde, the Victorian dandy, and we can conceptualize the nature of Rodman's performance if we think of him as an up-
dated version of the dandy. In his case, the more accurate label is "the
vulgar dandy," another contradiction in terms that is appropriate for
Rodman's self-construction. Though Rodman differs from the conventional dandy because he is lacking in taste, like the dandy he
plays his role with such virtuosity that it explodes the notion that
conventional social roles have any inherent meaning or natural au-
thority. The significance of this emphasis on performance rather than
the text itself—the social role and the supposedly inherent values
that sanction it—is that it symbolizes the uniqueness of the self. By
transforming his role as the cross-dressing, chameleon-haired basketball player whose body has been turned into a work of art of
unimagined flamboyance by its medley of musculature and tattoos
and piercings, he demonstrates the inadequacy of conventional society to comprehend the demands of the self.[12] When we think of Rodman's appearance, it is clear that one way he has created himself is
by literally "fashioning" himself, and the costume he wears on the
front and back jackets of *Bad as I Wanna Be* is so revealing that it does
not require clothes.

Like the dandy, Rodman sees his life in terms of art when he announces in the opening pages of *Bad as I Wanna Be*, "My story read
like fiction." But his model is not the novel. He is a visually oriented
child of the new media and conceptualizes his life as "a made-for-TV
special." As quoting the lyrics of Pearl Jam's "Alive" before beginning the first chapter of his life story suggests, the art form he most

11. Oscar Wilde, *Four Plays by Oscar Wilde*, 134. In act III of *A Woman of No Importance*, Lord Illingworth says, "Moderation is a fatal thing, Lady Hunstanton.
Nothing succeeds like excess."

12. I take this concept of the significance of the dandy from Morse Peckham's
essay, "The Dilemma of a Century: The Four Stages of Romanticism," in Peckham, ed. *Romanticism: The Culture of the Nineteenth Century*, 21–22, although from
Peckham's perspective, Rodman would also be what he defines as the virtuoso
because he transforms the role by excess.

identifies with is rock music. (He also takes the title of the next installment of his life story, *Walk on the Wild Side,* from a Lou Reed lyric.) Although he does mention his commitment to the team and to winning, what he emphasizes is that the National Basketball Association is a "stage" and his role is to provide "entertainment to the fans." He explains that, like Pearl Jam, "You have to have stage presence and emotion, and you have to be able to make the people watching feel what you feel." He realizes that it is not primarily his basketball skills that make him a celebrity. "I don't hear," he confesses, "'I think you're a great basketball player,'" but young fans admire him, he believes, because he's "cool" and they love his "style."[13]

We can place Rodman's performance in the American tradition of the Western frontiersman with his "barbaric yawp" and the "ringtail roarers" and their hyperbolic stories, but, as Rodman's explanation reveals, the difference is that he never forgets that he plays before the eye of the audience. "It's a show," he insists, "and if everybody's watching, I might as well be an actor."[14] As the trajectory of his basketball career took him from Detroit to San Antonio and Chicago, he confesses that "What I did . . . was totally change my persona, and the persona of the game changed with me." Changing his fluid identity meant essentially only changing his costume. He adds, "It was nothing to go from there to red hair, or orange hair, or green hair with the red AIDS ribbon colored into the back of my head." The more Rodman explains, the more absurd the self-image becomes. The weirdly appropriate metaphor he chooses to describe the defiance symbolized by the tattoos, hair coloring, and piercings is "coloring outside the lines," but he insists such actions were the reason he frightened the league because he was bringing to the game human "dignity"— another contradiction within a contradiction.[15]

Even the costume embodies contradictions. In *Walk on the Wild Side*—with this third autobiography within three years and a fourth to come, he's really tested "Nothing exceeds like excess" as well as proved Boorstin's thesis that repetition makes the hero but undoes the celebrity—he opens with a detailed description of his New Year's Eve outfit: "I'm dressed as a sort of psychedelic Cleopatra,

13. Rodman and Keown, *Bad as I Wanna Be,* 2, 59, 85, 101.
14. Rodman and Silver, *Walk on the Wild Side,* 127.
15. Rodman and Keown, *Bad as I Wanna Be,* 97.

complete with a gold gladiator's helmet, a purple-feather Mardi Gras mask, a jeweled necklace, a sparkling cape made of gold and purple sequins, a shield hanging over my private parts, and gold-painted, lace-up pumps." At first glance, the picture reinforces Rodman's subversive persona as a cross-dresser, but he carefully points out the masculine features of the costume: the gladiator's helmet and the sexually explicit "shield hanging over my privates." Rather than cross-dress in clearly feminine attire, he mixes the feminine and the masculine, creating, according to one scholar, "a pastiche of ambiguous gender codes." Again, the image Rodman creates is not content-less, but its significance lies in its surface gesture. It is another index to the postmodern celebrity. Rodman does, as he claims, "make himself," but he becomes typical of what Leo Braudy in his history of fame calls the modern "collage" personality. Braudy explains that the modern celebrity is "made up of fragments of public people who are, in turn, made from fragments themselves—polished, denatured, simplified."[16]

Rodman's Janus-like persona is replete with other contradictions. In choosing to perform "badness," Rodman associates himself with a particular image of blackness, one that encourages readers to identify him with the culture of "gangsta rap" and the black criminal. John Hoberman, for example, argues that the sports industry, the music industry, and the advertising industry have merged the black athlete with the gangster rapper and the criminal to create the predominant image of black masculinity.[17] Rodman confesses in *Bad as I Wanna Be*, however, "Black culture is something I don't relate to much at all," and he singles out "gangsta rap" as the main symbol of black culture. He rejects "gangsta rap" and similar aspects of black culture as being exploitative, and says he, on the contrary, identifies with Pearl Jam and, as he mentions in *Walk on the Wild Side,* with Elvis, Jim Morrison, Jimi Hendrix, and other musicians who played at Woodstock. It is hard to reconcile the image of the black sexual athlete who rides a Harley-Davidson with the shy person who confesses in *Walk on the Wild Side* that he didn't lose his virginity until he was

16. Rodman and Silver, *Walk on the Wild Side*, 2. Dunbar, "Dennis Rodman—Do You Feel Feminine Yet?" 270. Braudy, *The Frenzy of Renown*, 5.

17. John Hoberman, *Darwin's Athletes: How Sport Has Damaged Black America and Preserved the Myth of Race*, xviii.

20 or 21 and that his first musical loves were the Carpenters and the Captain and Tennille. But the issue goes beyond musical taste. He points out that most of his friends and his former wife are white, and most of the women he dates are white. More strikingly, he adds, "There were many times I thought I wanted to be white." Later he even drops the qualification, admits he wants to be white, and adds, "Black was never the right color."[18]

In a short profile in the *New Yorker,* novelist John Edgar Wideman's imaginative take on Rodman implicitly turns on the concept of paradox, a form of contradiction, even if Wideman's thesis unambiguously argues Rodman's essential and subversive blackness. Alluding to Shakespeare's *The Tempest* in calling Rodman Caliban to NBA Commissioner David Stern's authoritarian Prospero, Wideman draws upon black vernacular to get at Rodman's persona. He says that Rodman "embodies *'tain't,'*" which he defines as "a mysteriously alluring, unclassifiable, scary region between a woman's legs." (The etymology, Wideman explains, quoting Walter Bentley, is that it "'tain't pussy and 'tain't asshole, it's just the 'tain't.'")[19] Although Wideman doesn't point out the contradiction in using the female anatomy to describe a black male whom he also says is "cocksure" because of his displaced, pent-up energy, his conception of Rodman reinforces the playful cross-gender traits that form one side of Rodman's Janus self-construction.

The most revealing index of his ability to contain contradictions lies in his claims about the relationship between authenticity and celebrity. On the one hand, the recurring theme in *Bad as I Wanna Be, Walk on the Wild Side,* and *I Should Be Dead by Now* is his ability to maintain his personal integrity despite his celebrity status. He is a fatherless boy who has nevertheless been able to honor Polonius's advice to his son, "To thine own self be true." He contemptuously dismisses players like Grant Hill and other conservative role models he derides as "the NBA kids." These "poster child[ren]" have allowed the league to turn them into products and commodities. He, on the other hand, is unique, he insists, because he has proved that "you can be in the public spotlight and still be true to yourself." The

18. Rodman and Keown, *Bad as I Wanna Be,* 137, 135, 144.
19. John Edgar Wideman, "Playing Dennis Rodman," 94.

explanation is that the image he has constructed "is not an act BUT THE REAL ME."[20]

This is what in literary criticism is sometimes called self-dramatization—the author creates a persona that he encourages the reader to identify with himself—and it also became Rodman's approach to the MTV reality program, "Rodman World Tour." His performance on the show was always represented as "being himself," just as *Bad as I Wanna Be* characterizes his "unusual" actions such as dyeing his hair and wearing piercings and tattoos as "being his real self." The show was a pastiche of clips from other sources and video shot specifically for "Rodman World Tour." According to Michelle Dunbar's analysis, because it was "constructed as a window to reality while at the same time allowing the audience to see the constructed nature of the show," it "blur[red] the distinction between reality and fictional entertainment." The postmodern self has become the role. As a result, despite his criticism of "the NBA kids" as marketing shills for the league, he can say with pride, "I was like a new product, something the NBA had never seen before," and explain cross-dressing as giving the fans "the whole package." In the contemporary world of sports as well as in the larger society, Dennis Rodman represents the latest version of the American story of the "self-made man": the self as commodity to be packaged for the public. Like many celebrity athletes, Rodman made more money from endorsements than from this salary as a player. In the late 1990s, for example, Rodman had contracts with Nike, Pizza Pizza, Converse, Kodak, McDonald's, Victoria's Secret, Mystic Beverages, a national hotel chain, several clothing store chains, multinational computer companies, and was negotiating with Walt Disney Productions and Warner Brothers for the film rights to *Bad as I Wanna Be*.[21]

- **A Two-Part Obituary**

Like other Janus figures, Dennis Rodman is not just a figure of contradictions but also lends himself to opposing interpretations. Some

20. William Shakespeare, *Hamlet*, 203. Polonius is speaking to his son Laertes in act I, scene 3, line 78. Rodman and Keown, *Bad as I Wanna Be*, 56, 102. Rodman and Silver, *Walk on the Wild Side*, 11.

21. Dunbar, "Dennis Rodman—Do You Feel Feminine Yet?" 269, 268, 272. Rodman and Keown, *Bad as I Wanna Be*, 35, 178. Lafrance and Rail, "Excursions into Otherness," 46.

cultural commentators might choose to construct the following "obituary" for him:

In American folklore and literature the legend of the hero is complemented by the tale of the trickster. Guile and cunning were one of many expressions of the pluck Americans would use instead of the entitlements of rank to make their destinies. The evolution of the trickster from the nineteenth to the twenty-first century follows a route that branches in interesting and sometimes bizarre directions. The leap from the carnival world of P. T. Barnum to the marquee of the NBA is not a large one. It tracks the increasing movement of sport toward the tents of business and entertainment.

Dennis Rodman is a latter-day P. T. Barnum, both the exhibit and the carnival barker at the same time. Like Barnum's prodigies, he may be a wonder, but he can be only a "three-day wonder." He is the modern celebrity who tells us who we are by acting out some of our fantasies. But he poses no real questions; he merely poses. He is the flamboyant poseur, striking but static. Unlike the hero, he is doomed to repeat himself in ways that diminish rather than enlarge him. His 1998 marriage to a starlet—the diminutive term is instructive—on the television show *Baywatch* could only be a contraction of his previous sensational affair with Madonna. The chapter in *Bad as I Wanna Be* about the championships he won with the Bulls is entitled "When the Circus Comes to Chicago," but his attempt to repeat his act in Los Angeles was only a pale cameo and when he was released by the Lakers he left with a whimper not a bang. His final act was a fitting one; he was reincarnated as a professional wrestler named "Rodzilla," an athlete who only struts the stage rather than competes. Rodman is right when he boasts, "I made myself." But, as Boorstin predicts, it was time that unmade him. The fate of the celebrity is to tell us, among other things, that it is not always the favorites of the gods who die young.

But other commentators might be more sympathetic to the contemporary celebrity and the irony that often informs his performance. Another self-dramatizing, self-confessed showman, Lord Byron, described his greatest poem, *Don Juan*, as "A versified Aurora Borealis, / Which flashes o'er a waste and icy clime" (Canto VII, stanza 2, lines 3–4).[22] Like Rodman, Byron was also writing at a time of crisis in culture in which all the old certainties and verities seemed

---

22. Byron, *The Poetical Works of Byron*, 867.

passing away, and the only sane response to life, Byron argues, is an ironic awareness and one of the few values he affirms is the same one that Rodman celebrates: personal freedom. The hero of Byron's poem—a term he used ironically in an age when, he wrote, "every year and month sends forth a new one" (Canto I, stanza 1, line 2)—is someone who "was what / [Women] pleased to make or take him for" (Canto XV, stanza 16, lines 1–2). Because Juan has mastered the "art of living in all climes with ease" (Canto XV, stanza 11, line 8),[23] he anticipates the kind of fluid, protean self that Rodman and other postmodern celebrities now model as the fashion of our times. While others find a world without ultimate truths anxiety-producing, Byron and his descendants see this same world as giving us the freedom to live without the burden of ultimate truths. The dandy's insouciance and posing, the Janus figure's self-contradictions, the celebrity's self-dramatization and costumes are all gestures about the value of the individual and of freedom. The sense of the absurdity of it all can be liberating.

It would also be absurd to credit Rodman with this kind of metaphysical awareness, but it is not too much of a stretch to find some of its implications in his performance. As I have argued, the self he presents is a collage and a pastiche, not a monolithic whole. As he proclaims, he is "the Madonna of the NBA." It is this construction of a shifting, kaleidoscopic self that John Edgar Wideman recognizes when he describes him as "a perpetual work in progress, compelling, outrageous, amoral." In a culture in which we must speak not of *the* audience but of fragmented *audiences,* the celebrity as collage reflects that reality. According to Garry Whannel, we must repose the question of who are our heroes? and ask, heroes for whom? The anomalous fragments in the collage respond to the diverse "expectations of those who want a role model . . . and those for whom sport is an entertaining soap opera." While we may nostalgically wish for heroes who represented the dilated self, Leo Braudy argues that the contemporary celebrity is an "extended self." Athletes, movie stars, and politicians are certainly not normal members of society, but they are "extensions of everyone's culturally fostered desire to be given his or her due." When Rodman explains that for him cross-dressing

23. Ibid., 747, 970, 969.

is "total freedom," the "freedom to be who the fuck you want to be," his ideal is an extension of the desire that we all feel. It also supports Braudy's view that in Western society the dream of fame has always been "inseparable from the ideal of personal freedom." But in contemporary culture the pressures of the corporate mentality, conformity, and other threats to individuality force the celebrity to choose ever more bizarre costumes. In the case of Rodman's crossdressing, we have a costumed celebrity who exemplifies Braudy's thesis that fame now entails "the paradoxical modern sense of simultaneously being venerated and trivialized"—as well as another explanation of Rodman's Janus-like self.[24]

Like other public figures who write autobiographies—let alone publish four by the time they are little more than forty years old—Rodman has motives that clearly include the desire to memorialize himself. What gives this desire its distinctively modern cast is that the current cultural situation is a world without an afterlife. This reality determines Rodman's conception of personal immortality. In *Walk on the Wild Side*, he describes his image of the appropriate final resting place: "When I die, I want to be stripped naked, frozen, and placed in a see-through freezer. I want to be put on display—in my house, or maybe in some sort of museum—so people can come by and check me out forevermore." Rodman's motto is "different is better," but this is a bizarre image of the fish out of water. Although the grotesqueness and vulgarity of the image are not incidental details, the dominant point of Rodman's fantasy exemplifies Braudy's thesis that, in the "democratic theater" of America, "[t]o be seen was to be free, to be heroic, to be American."[25] Here is the postmodern celebrity imagining a bizarre personal immortality in which even after death he continues to perform at the center of the stage, a celebrity who has to do nothing but simply be himself.

24. Rodman and Keown, *Bad as I Wanna Be*, 146, 180. Wideman, "Playing Dennis Rodman," 94. Garry Whannel, *Media Sport Stars: Masculinities and Moralities*, 45, 47. Braudy, *The Frenzy of Renown*, 5, 7, 454.

25. Rodman and Silver, *Walk on the Wild Side*, 190. Rodman and Keown, *Bad as I Wanna Be*, 94. Braudy, *The Frenzy of Renown*, 453.

Aaron, Hank, and Lonnie Wheeler. *I Had a Hammer: The Hank Aaron Story*. New York: Harper Paperbacks, 1992. The autobiography was originally published by Harper-Collins (New York) in 1991.

Abdul-Jabbar, Kareem, and Peter Knobler. *Giant Steps: The Autobiography of Kareem Abdul-Jabbar*. New York: Bantam Books, 1983.

Abrams, M. H. *Natural Supernaturalism: Tradition and Revolution in Romantic Literature*. New York: W. W. Norton and Company, Inc., 1971.

Ali, Muhammad, and Richard Durham. *The Greatest: My Own Story*. New York: Random House, 1975.

Alzado, Lyle, and Paul Lionel Zimmerman. *Mile High: The Story of Lyle Alzado and the Amazing Denver Broncos*. New York: Atheneum, 1978.

Andrews, David L., and Steven J. Jackson, eds. *Sport Stars: The Cultural Politics of Sporting Celebrity*. London and New York: Routledge, 2001.

Austin, Tracy, and Christine Brennan. *Beyond Center Court: My Story*. New York: William Morrow and Company, Inc., 1992.

Baker, Aaron, and Todd Boyd. *Out of Bounds: Sports Media and the Politics of Identity*. Bloomington: Indiana University Press, 1997.

Barkley, Charles, and Roy S. Johnson. *Outrageous!: The Fine Life and Flagrant Good Times of Basketball's Irresistible Force*. New York: Avon Books, 1993. The autobiography was originally published by Simon and Schuster (New York) in 1992.

Barry, Rick, and Bill Libby. *Confessions of a Basketball Gypsy: The Rick Barry Story*. Englewood Cliffs, N.J.: Prentice Hall, Inc., 1972.

Benoit, Joan, and Sally Baker. *Running Tide.* New York: Alfred A. Knopf, 1987.

Bird, Larry, and Bob Ryan. *Drive: The Story of My Life.* New York: Doubleday, 1989.

Birrell, Susan, and Mary G. McDonald, eds. *Reading Sport: Critical Essays on Power and Representation.* Boston: Northeastern University Press, 2000.

Blake, William. *Selected Poetry and Prose of Blake.* Edited by Northrop Frye. New York: Modern Library, 1953.

Boorstin, Daniel J. *The Image: A Guide to Pseudo-Events in America.* New York: Vintage Books, 1992.

Bouton, Jim, and Leonard Shecter. *Ball Four.* Twentieth Anniversary Edition. New York: Collier Books, 1995. The autobiography was originally published by World Publishing Company (New York) in 1970.

Boyd, Todd. "The Day the Niggaz Took Over: Basketball, Commodity Culture, and Black Masculinity." In Aaron Baker and Todd Boyd, eds., *Out of Bounds: Sports Media and the Politics of Identity* (Bloomington: Indiana University Press, 1997), 123–42.

Bradley, Bill. *Life on the Run.* New York: Vintage Books, 1995. The diary was originally published by Quadrangle (New York) in 1976.

Braudy, Leo. *The Frenzy of Renown: Fame and Its History.* New York: Oxford University Press, 1986.

Brisman, Leslie. *Romantic Origins.* Ithaca, N.Y.: Cornell University Press, 1978.

Brodie, John, and James D. Houston. *Open Field.* Boston: Houghton Mifflin, 1974.

Brosnan, Jim. *The Long Season.* Evanston, Ill.: Holtzman Press, Inc., 1960.

Brown, Jim, and Steve Delsohn. *Out of Bounds.* New York: Zebra Books, Kensington Publishing Corp., 1989.

Browning, Robert. *Robert Browning: Selected Poetry.* New York: Holt, Rinehart and Winston, 1964.

Byron, George Gordon. *The Poetical Works of Byron.* Cambridge Edition. Boston: Houghton Mifflin Company, 1975.

Cayleff, Susan E. *Babe: The Life and Legend of Babe Didrikson Zaharias.* Urbana: University of Illinois Press, 1995.

————. "The 'Texas Tomboy': The Life and Legend of Babe Didrikson Zaharias." *Organization of American Historians Magazine of History* 7 (Summer 1992): 28–33.

Chamberlain, Wilt, and David Shaw. *Wilt: Just Like Any Other 7-Foot Black Millionaire Who Lives Next Door.* New York: Macmillan Publishing Co., Inc., 1973.

Chandler, Bob, and Norm Chandler Fox. *Violent Sundays.* New York: A Fireside Book, Simon and Schuster, Inc., 1984.

Chawaf, Chantal. "Linguistic Flesh." Translated by Yvonne Rochette-Ozzello. In Elaine Marks and Isabelle de Courtivron, eds., *New French Feminisms: An Anthology* (New York: Schocken, 1981), 177–78.

Cobb, Ty, and Al Stump. *My Life in Baseball: The True Record.* Lincoln: University of Nebraska Press, 1993. The autobiography was originally published by Doubleday (New York) in 1961.

Conrad, Joseph. *Youth and Two Other Stories.* Malay Edition. Garden City, N.Y.: Doubleday, Doran and Company, Inc., 1928.

Cousy, Bob, and Ed Linn. *The Last Loud Roar.* Englewood Cliffs, N.J.: Prentice Hall, 1964.

Crepeau, Richard C. "Sport, Heroes and Myth." *Journal of Sport and Social Issues* 4 (Fall/Winter 1980): 23–31.

Dempsey, Jack, and Barbara Piattelli Dempsey. *Dempsey.* New York: Harper and Row, 1977.

DiMaggio Joe. *Lucky to Be a Yankee.* New York: Rudolph Field, 1946.

Ditka, Mike, and Don Pierson. *Ditka: An Autobiography.* Chicago: Bonus Books, 1986.

DuBois, W. E. B. *The Souls of Black Folk.* New York: Bantam Books, 1989.

Dunbar, Michelle. "Dennis Rodman—Do You Feel Feminine Yet?: Black Masculinity, Gender Transgression, and Reproductive Rebellion on MTV." In Jim McKay, Michael A. Messner, and Don Sabo, eds., *Masculinities, Gender Relations, and Sport* (Thousand Oaks, Calif.: Sage Publications Inc., 2000), 263–85.

Early, Gerald. *The Culture of Bruising: Essays on Prizefighting, Literature, and Modern American Culture.* Hopewell, N.J.: Ecco Press, 1994.

Eitzen, D. Stanley. *Fair and Foul: Beyond the Myths and Paradoxes of Sport.* Lanham, Md.: Roman and Littlefield Publishers, Inc., 1999.

Eliade, Mircea. *Rites and Symbols of Initiation: The Mysteries of Birth and Rebirth.* Translated by Willard R. Trask. Woodstock, Conn.: Spring Publications, 1995.

Eliot, T. S. *The Complete Poems and Plays, 1909–1950.* New York: Harcourt, Brace and World, Inc., 1971.

Fiedler, Leslie. *Freaks: Myths and Images of the Secret Self.* New York: Simon and Schuster, 1978.

Fitzgerald, F. Scott. *The Crack-Up.* Edited by Edmund Wilson. New York: New Directions Books, 1945.

Ford, Whitey, and Phil Pepe. *Slick.* New York: William Morrow and Company, Inc., 1987.

Frazier, Joe, and Phil Berger. *Smokin' Joe: The Autobiography of a Heavyweight Champion of the World, Smokin' Joe Frazier.* New York: Macmillan, 1996.

Frost, Robert. *The Poetry of Robert Frost.* Edited by Edward Connery Lathem. New York: Holt, Rinehart and Winston, 1967.

Gallop, Jane. *Thinking Through the Body.* New York: Columbia University Press, 1988.

Garfield, Ken. "Chip Hilton Series Makes a Return." *Charlotte Observer,* November 21, 1998. Available online at: http://www.texnews.com/1998/religion/garf1121.html.

Garvey, Steve, and Skip Rozin. *Garvey.* New York: New York Times Books, 1986.

Gent, Peter. *North Dallas Forty.* New York: William Morrow, 1973.

Giamatti, A. Bartlett. *Take Time for Paradise: Americans and Their Games.* New York: Summit Books, 1989.

Gibson, Althea, and Ed Fitzgerald. *I Always Wanted to Be Somebody.* New York: Harper, 1958.

Gibson, Bob, and Lonnie Wheeler. *Stranger to the Game: The Autobiography of Bob Gibson.* New York: Penguin Books, 1996. The autobiography was first published by Viking (New York) in 1994.

Gilmore, Leigh. *The Limits of Autobiography: Trauma and Testimony.* Ithaca, N.Y.: Cornell University Press, 2001.

Gladwell, Malcolm. "Physical Genius." *New Yorker* 75, no. 21 (August 2, 1999): 56–65.

Graziano, Rocky, and Rowland Barber. *Somebody Up There Likes Me: The Story of My Life until Today.* New York: Simon and Schuster, 1954.

Grier, Roosevelt "Rosey," and Dennis Baker. *Rosey: The Gentle Giant.* Tulsa, Okla.: Honors Books, Harrison House, 1986.

Guttmann, Allen. *From Ritual to Record: The Nature of Modern Sports.* New York: Columbia University Press, 1978.

———. *A Whole New Ball Game: An Interpretation of American Sports.* Chapel Hill: University of North Carolina Press, 1988.

———. *Women's Sports: A History.* New York: Columbia University Press, 1991.

Haywood, Spencer, and Scott Osler. *Spencer Haywood: The Rise, the Fall, the Recovery.* New York: Amistad, 1992.

Hoberman, John. *Darwin's Athletes: How Sport Has Damaged Black America and Preserved the Myth of Race.* Boston: Houghton Mifflin, 1997.

Huey, Lynda. *A Running Start: An Athlete, A Woman.* New York: Quadrangle/New York Times Book Co., 1976.

Jackson, Reggie, and Mike Lupica. *Reggie: The Autobiography.* New York: Villard Books, 1984.

Jefferson, Margo. "Dennis Rodman, Bad Boy as Man of the Moment." *New York Times,* January 30, 1997, C13, C20.

Johnson, Earvin "Magic," and William Novak. *My Life.* New York: Fawcett Cress, 1993.

Johnson, Jack. *Jack Johnson—in the Ring—and Out.* Chicago: National Sports Publishing Company, 1927.

Johnson, Steve. "Trash Talk." *Chicago Tribune,* December 1996 (online). Available: http://www.chicago.tribune.com/sports/bulls/belndr/bsrchive/rod61205.htm.

Jordan, Pat. *A False Spring.* St. Paul, Minn.: Hungry Mind Press, 1998. The autobiography was originally published by Dodd, Mead (New York) in 1975.

———. *After the Sundown.* New York: Dodd, Mead and Company, 1979.

Justice, Richard. "Life after Football: Hello, Real World." *Houston Chronicle,* January 31, 2004, 1B, 15B.

Kahn, Roger. *The Boys of Summer.* New York: Harper and Row, 1972.

———. "Intellectuals and Ballplayers." *American Scholar* 26 (Summer 1957): 342–49.

Kazin, Alfred. "The Self as History: Reflections on Autobiography." In Albert E. Stone, ed., *The American Autobiography: A Collection of Critical Essays* (Englewood Cliffs, N.J.: Prentice Hall, 1981), 31–43.

Keats, John. *Complete Poems and Selected Letters of John Keats.* New York: Modern Library, 2001.

King, Billie Jean, and Frank Deford. *Billie Jean.* New York: Viking Press, 1982.

Kopay, Dave, and Perry Deane Young. *The Dave Kopay Story: An Extraordinary Self-Revelation.* New York: Arbor House, 1977.

Kramer, Jerry, and Dick Schaap. *Instant Replay: The Green Bay Diary of Jerry Kramer.* New York: New American Library, 1968.

Kunitz, Stanley. *Next-to-Last Things: New Poems and Essays.* Boston: Atlantic Monthly Press, 1985.

Lafrance, Mélisse, and Geneviève Rail. "As Bad as He Says He Is?: Interrogating Dennis Rodman's Subversive Potential." In Susan Birrell and Mary G. McDonald, eds., *Reading Sport: Critical Essays on Power and Representation* (Boston: Northeastern University Press, 2000), 74–107.

———. "Excursions into Otherness: Understanding Dennis Rodman and the Limits of Subversive Agency." In David L. Andrews and Steven J. Jackson, eds., *Sport Stars: The Cultural Politics of Sporting Celebrity* (London and New York: Routledge, 2001), 36–50.

La Motta, Jake, Joseph Carter, and Peter Savage. *Raging Bull: The True Story of a Champ.* New York: Bantam Books, 1980. The autobiography was originally published by Prentice Hall (New York) in 1970.

Lasch, Christopher. "The Corruption of Sports." In Wiley Lee Umphlett, ed., *American Sport Culture: The Humanistic Dimensions* (Lewisburg, Pa.: Bucknell University Press, 1985), 50–67.

Leibowitz, Herbert. *Fabricating Lives: Explorations in American Autobiography.* New York: Alfred A. Knopf, 1989.

Lipsyte, John. "Varsity Syndrome: The Unkindest Cut." In Wiley Lee Umphlett, ed., *American Sport Culture: The Humanistic Dimensions* (Lewisburg, Pa.: Bucknell University Press, 1985), 111–21.

Lloyd, Chris Evert, and Neil Amdur. *Chrissie: My Own Story.* New York: Simon and Schuster, 1982.

Lopez, Nancy, and Peter Schwed. *The Education of a Woman Golfer.* New York: Simon and Schuster, 1979.

Louganis, Greg, and Eric Marcus. *Breaking the Surface.* New York: Plume Books, 1996. The autobiography was originally published by Random House (New York) in 1995.

Louis, Joe, and Edna and Art Rust, Jr. *Joe Louis: My Life.* Hopewell, N.J.: Ecco Press, 1997. The autobiography was originally published by Harcourt, Brace, Jovanovich (New York) in 1978.

Lowenthal, Leo. *Literature, Popular Culture, and Society.* Englewood Cliffs, N.J.: Prentice Hall, Inc., 1961.

Lucas, John, and Joseph Moriarity. *Winning a Day at a Time.* Center City, Minn.: Hazelden Educational Materials, 1994.

Mantle, Mickey, and Herb Gluck. *The Mick.* Garden City, N.Y.: Doubleday, 1985.

Marble, Alice, and Dale Leatherman. *Courting Danger: My Adventures in World-Class Tennis, Golden-Age Hollywood, and High-Stakes Spying.* New York: St. Martin's Press, 1991.

Marks, Elaine, and Isabelle de Courtivron, eds. *New French Feminisms: An Anthology.* New York: Schocken, 1981.

Mathews, Eddie, and Bob Buege. *Eddie Mathews and the National Pastime.* Milwaukee: Douglas American Sports Publications, 1994.

May, Rollo. *Love and Will.* New York: W. W. Norton and Company, Inc., 1969.

Mays, Willie, and Lou Sahadi. *Say Hey: The Autobiography of Willie Mays.* New York: Pocket Books, 1989.

McCormick, Patricia. *Lady Bullfighter: The Autobiography of the North American Matador.* New York: Henry Holt and Company, 1954.

McKay, Jim, Michael A. Messner, and Don Sabo, eds. *Masculinities, Gender Relations, and Sport.* Thousand Oaks, Calif.: Sage Publications, Inc., 2000.

Meggysey, Dave. *Out of Their League.* New York: Paperback Library, 1971. The autobiography was originally published by Ramparts (Berkeley, Calif.) in 1970.

Messenger, Christian K. *Sport and the Spirit of Play in American Fiction: Hawthorne to Faulkner.* New York: Columbia University Press, 1981.

Mikan, George L., and Joseph Oberle. *Unstoppable: The Story of George Mikan, the First NBA Superstar.* Indianapolis: Masters Press, 1997.

Navratilova, Martina, and George Vecsey. *Martina.* New York: Fawcett Cress, 1985. The autobiography was originally published by Knopf (New York) in 1985.

Neuman, Shirley, ed. *Autobiography and Questions of Gender.* London: Frank Cass, 1991.

Nicklaus, Jack, and Ken Bowden. *Jack Nicklaus: My Story.* New York: Fireside, 1998.

Novak, Michael. "American Sports, American Virtues." In Wiley Lee Umphlett, ed., *American Sport Culture: The Humanistic Dimensions* (Lewisburg, Pa.: Bucknell University Press, 1985), 34–49.

———. *The Joy of Sports: End Zones, Bases, Baskets, Balls, and the Consecration of the American Spirit.* New York: Basic Books, Inc., 1976.

Nyad, Diana. *Other Shores.* New York: Random House, 1978.

Offen, Neil. *God Save the Players: The Funny, Crazy, Sometimes Violent World of Sports Fans.* Chicago: Playboy Press, 1974.

Olajuwon, Hakeem, and Peter Knobler. *Living the Dream: My Life and Basketball.* Boston: Little, Brown, 1996.

Oliver, Chip, and Ron Rapoport. *High for the Game.* New York: William Morrow and Company, 1971.

O'Loughlin, Michael. *The Garlands of Repose: The Literary Celebration of Civic and Retired Leisure.* Chicago: University of Chicago Press, 1978.

Oriard, Michael. *The End of Autumn: Reflections on My Life in Football.* Garden City, N.Y.: Doubleday and Company, Inc., 1982.

Paige, Leroy Satchel, and Hal Lebovitz. *Pitchin' Man: Satchel Paige's Own Story.* Westport, Conn.: Meckler, 1948.

Pascal, Roy. *Design and Truth in Autobiography.* Cambridge, Mass.: Harvard University Press, 1960.

Peckham, Morse, ed. *Romanticism: The Culture of the Nineteenth Century.* New York: George Brazlier, 1965.

———. *The Triumph of Romanticism.* Columbia: University of South Carolina Press, 1970.

Pettit, Bob, and Bob Wolff. *Bob Pettit: The Drive within Me.* Englewood Cliffs, N.J.: Prentice Hall, 1966.

Pfister, Joel. *The Production of Personal Life: Class, Gender, and the Psychological in Hawthorne's Fiction.* Stanford, Calif.: Stanford University Press, 1991.

Piersall, Jim, and Al Hirshberg. *Fear Strikes Out: The Jim Piersall Story.* Boston: Little, Brown, 1955.

Pipkin, James W. "Life on the Cusp: Lynda Huey and Billie Jean King." In Avital H. Bloch and Lauri Umansky, eds., *Impossible to Hold: Women and Culture in the 1960s* (New York: New York University Press, 2005), 43–64.

Pope, Alexander. *Pastoral Poetry and An Essay on Criticism.* Edited by E. Audra and Aubrey Williams. Vol. 1 of *The Poems of Alexander Pope.* London: Methuen and Co. Ltd. and New Haven, Conn.: Yale University Press, 1954.

Porter, Roger J. "Figuration and Disfigurement: Herculine Barbin and the Autobiography of the Body." In Shirley Neuman, ed., *Autobiography and Questions of Gender* (London: Frank Cass, 1991), 122–36.

"Professors Call for Papers on Basketball's Dennis Rodman." *Chronicle of Higher Education* (October 18, 1996): A18.

Rader, Benjamin G. "Compensatory Sport Heroes: Ruth, Grange and Dempsey." *Journal of Popular Culture* 16 (Spring 1983): 11–22.

Rentzel, Lance. *When All the Laughter Died in Sorrow.* New York: Saturday Review Press, 1972.

Retton, Mary Lou, Bela Karolyi, and John Powers. *Mary Lou: Creating an Olympic Champion.* New York: McGraw-Hill Book Company, 1986.

Robinson, Jackie, and Alfred Duckett. *I Never Had It Made: An Autobiography.* Hopewell, N.J.: Ecco Press, 1995. The autobiography was originally published by Putnam (New York) in 1972.

Rodman, Dennis, and Tim Keown. *Bad as I Wanna Be.* New York: Delacourt Press, 1996.

———, and Jack Isenhour. *I Should Be Dead by Now.* Champaign, Ill.: Sports Publishing L.L.C., 2005.

———, Pat Rich, and Alan Steinberg. *Rebound: The Dennis Rodman Story.* New York: Crown Publishers, Inc., 1994.

———, and Michael Silver. *Walk on the Wild Side.* New York: Delacorte, 1997.

Rousseau, Jean-Jacques. *The First and Second Discourses.* Edited by Roger D. Masters. New York: St. Martin's Press, 1964.

Russell, Bill, and Taylor Branch. *Second Wind: The Memoirs of an Opinionated Man.* New York: Random House, 1979.

Ruth, Babe, and Bob Considine. *The Babe Ruth Story.* New York: Scholastic Book Services, 1948.

Ryan, Nolan, and Harvey Frommer. *Throwing Heat: The Autobiography of Nolan Ryan*. New York: Avon Books, 1990. The autobiography was originally published by Doubleday (New York) in 1988.

Shakespeare, William. *Hamlet*. The Arden Edition of the Works of William Shakespeare. Edited by Harold Jenkins. London and New York: Methuen, 1982.

————. *The Tempest*. Edited by Frank Kermode. Cambridge, Mass.: Harvard University Press, 1958.

Shriver, Pam, Frank Deford, and Susan B. Adams. *Passing Shots: Pam Shriver on Tour*. New York: McGraw-Hill Book Company, 1987.

Smith, Gary. "Moment of Truth." *Sports Illustrated* 91, no. 4 (July 26, 1999): 133–49.

Spacks, Patricia Meyer. "Stages of Self: Notes on Autobiography and the Life Cycle." In Albert E. Stone, ed., *The American Autobiography: A Collection of Critical Essays* (Englewood Cliffs, N.J.: Prentice Hall, 1981), 44–60.

Spivey, Donald, ed. *Sport in America: New Historical Perspectives*. Westport, Conn.: Greenwood Press, 1985.

Stone, Albert E., ed. *The American Autobiography: A Collection of Critical Essays*. Englewood Cliffs, N.J.: Prentice Hall, 1981.

Taylor, Lawrence, and David Falkner. *LT: Living on the Edge*. New York: Times Books, Random House, 1987.

Tennyson, Alfred. *Selected Poetry of Tennyson*. Edited by Douglas Bush. New York: Modern Library, 1951.

Thomson, Rosemarie Garland. *Extraordinary Bodies: Figuring Physical Disability in American Culture and Literature*. New York: Columbia University Press, 1997.

Tilden, William T., 2nd. *My Story: A Champion's Memoirs*. New York: Hellman, Williams and Company, 1948.

Twin, Stephanie L. "Women and Sport." In Donald Spivey, ed., *Sport in America: New Historical Perspectives* (Westport, Conn.: Greenwood Press, 1985), 193–217.

Umphlett, Wiley Lee, ed. *American Sport Culture: The Humanistic Dimensions*. Lewisburg, Pa.: Bucknell University Press, 1985.

Unitas, Johnny, and Ed Fitzgerald. *Pro Quarterback: My Own Story*. New York: Simon and Schuster, 1965.

Walker, Chet, and Chris Messenger. *Long Time Coming: A Black Athlete's Coming-of-Age in America*. New York: Grove Press, 1995.

Walton, Bill, and Gene Wojciechowski. *Nothing but Net: Just Give Me the Ball and Get Out of the Way.* New York: Hyperion, 1994.

West, Jerry, and Bill Libby. *Mr. Clutch: The Jerry West Story.* Englewood Cliffs, N.J.: Prentice Hall, 1969.

West, Thomas G. *Plato's Apology of Socrates: An Interpretation, with a New Translation.* Ithaca, N.Y.: Cornell University Press, 1979.

Whannel, Garry. *Media Sport Stars: Masculinities and Moralities.* London and New York: Routledge, 2002.

Whitman, Walt. *Leaves of Grass.* Edited by Harold W. Blodgett and Sculley Bradley. New York: W. W. Norton and Company, Inc., 1965.

Wideman, John Edgar. "Playing Dennis Rodman." *New Yorker* 72, no. 10 (April 29 and May 6, 1996): 94–95.

Wilde, Oscar. *Four Plays by Oscar Wilde.* London: Unicorn Press, 1944.

Williams, Ted, and John Underwood. *My Turn at Bat: The Story of My Life.* New York: Simon and Schuster, 1988. The autobiography was originally published in 1969.

Wordsworth, William. *The Poetical Works of Wordsworth.* Cambridge Edition. Boston: Houghton Mifflin Company, 1982.

Yastrzemski, Carl, and Gerald Eskenazi. *Yaz: Baseball, the Wall, and Me.* New York: Doubleday, 1990.

Yeats, William Butler. *Selected Poems and Two Plays of William Butler Yeats.* Edited by M. L. Rosenthal. New York: Collier Books, 1962.

Zaharias, Babe Didrikson, and Harvey Paxton. *This Life I've Led.* New York: A. S. Barnes, 1955.